Protect Your Child

from

Bullying

Protect Your Child
from
Bullying

Expert Advice to Help You Recognize, Prevent, and Stop Bullying Before Your Child Gets Hurt

Allan L. Beane

JOSSEY-BASS
A Wiley Imprint
www.josseybass.com

Published by Jossey-Bass
A Wiley Imprint
989 Market Street, San Francisco, CA 94103-1741—www.josseybass.com

Readers should be aware that Internet web sites offered as citations and/or sources for further information may have changed or disappeared between the time this was written and when it is read.

Limit of Liability/Disclaimer of Warranty: While the publisher and author have used their best efforts in preparing this book, they make no representations or warranties with respect to the accuracy or completeness of the contents of this book and specifically disclaim any implied warranties of merchantability or fitness for a particular purpose. No warranty may be created or extended by sales representatives or written sales materials. The advice and strategies contained herein may not be suitable for your situation. You should consult with a professional where appropriate. Neither the publisher nor author shall be liable for any loss of profit or any other commercial damages, including but not limited to special, incidental, consequential, or other damages.

Jossey-Bass books and products are available through most bookstores. To contact Jossey-Bass directly call our Customer Care Department within the U.S. at 800-956-7739, outside the U.S. at 317-572-3986, or fax 317-572-4002.

Jossey-Bass also publishes its books in a variety of electronic formats. Some content that appears in print may not be available in electronic books.

Library of Congress Cataloging-in-Publication Data has been applied for.

8572

ISBN: 978-07879-95171

Printed in the United States of America
FIRST EDITION
PB Printing   10 9 8 7 6 5 4 3 2 1

CONTENTS

This book is dedicated to our son, Curtis Allan Beane, who was bullied in seventh grade and high school. It is also dedicated to our daughter, Christy Turner; our son-in-law, Mike Turner; and our grandchildren, Emily Grace Turner, Sarah Gail Turner, and Jacob Allan Turner. They have been the light in the darkness caused by Curtis's death. I hope this book and those who use it will bring light into the darkness of children who are mistreated.

PREFACE

Several years ago, the pain of being mistreated visited our home. When our son, Curtis, was in seventh grade, he was bullied and eventually isolated by several students. My wife and I decided to transfer him to another school system. He found acceptance and a sense of belonging at the new middle school. However, at age fifteen Curtis was in a car accident that changed his life.

My wife and I had to give the surgeons permission to remove two fingers and one-third of his right hand. He had two other fingers repaired and one rebuilt. When he went back to school, many of his classmates encouraged and supported him. Unfortunately, many were cruel to him. Once again, I asked myself, "How can kids be so cruel?" There was a cry from within me for answers. I wanted to know if I could stop cruelty from developing, and I wanted to stop it after it had already developed.

There was also a cry from within my son, but it was deeper and more intense than mine. The bullying had a tremendous impact on his self-esteem, confidence, and emotional health even into the adult years. At the age of twenty-three, he suffered from depression and anxiety. He developed posttraumatic stress from the car wreck and from the persistent peer mistreatment. He also sought the company of the wrong people. He got desperate to escape his pain by taking an illegal drug. He had a heart problem that no one knew about, and the drug killed him.

Now you understand why I am passionate about preventing and stopping bullying and why I am writing this book for you, the parents. I understand the pain expressed by children who are mistreated and the heartache experienced by their parents. I want to stop the pain.

Please join me in bringing light into the darkness of kids who are mistreated every day. I hope that you and your family are blessed with health, peace, and happiness and that you will act as instruments in promoting acceptance and a sense of belonging in others. Any child I can help through the actions of you and your family will bring honor and purpose to my son's life.

Bullying can be found in every neighborhood, school system, and school. To prevent and reduce bullying, a systematic effort must be made in each school. There must be a systemwide commitment to prevent and stop bullying. There must also be adult involvement, including parents and others in the community. This kind of commitment doesn't always exist. It is difficult to believe, but I have actually had school superintendents tell me that bullying didn't exist in their school system. Adults denying that bullying exists or ignoring bullying is the worst thing that can happen to children, a school, and a community. When adults get involved and harness the energy of school personnel, parents, community representatives, and children, bullying can be prevented and stopped, or at least significantly reduced. I often wonder if we can ever eliminate it—considering the nature of human beings. However, I am extremely hopeful.

I hope you find this book informative and helpful. It should help prevent your children from becoming victims of mistreatment and, if they are being mistreated, give them and you hope that the bullying will stop and that they will go on to lead happy, fulfilling lives.

Allan L. Beane

ACKNOWLEDGMENTS

Grateful thanks are offered to everyone who has helped by providing advice, information, and comments during the preparation of this book. Special acknowledgment and thanks are due to my wife, Linda Beane, for her proofreading and her desktop publishing knowledge and skills. I also appreciate her insight, love, and support during this project. Special thanks are also due to Darlene Gibson for her thorough proofreading of an earlier manuscript. I want to express my sincere gratitude to Kate Bradford, senior editor at Jossey-Bass. I thank her for her editorial assistance, knowledge, skills, ideas, and encouragement and support during the preparation of this manuscript.

ABOUT THE AUTHOR

Allan L. Beane, PhD, is an internationally recognized expert, speaker, and author on bullying, as well as a nationally renowned consultant and educator. He is the president of Bully Free Systems, LLC, in Murray, Kentucky. He has over thirty years' experience in education that includes teaching special education, teaching regular education, serving as vice president of a university, and serving as director of a school safety center. He has served as a consultant in criminal cases and lawsuits involving bullying and has been an expert guest on several television shows. He and material from his anti-bullying program have been featured in such national publications as USA Today, USA Weekend, Time for Kids, and Newsweek for Teens, and in many other national magazines and journals.

Dr. Beane's son was bullied in seventh grade and high school. His son's life inspired him to develop the Bully Free Program, which has been adopted around the United States. His first book, The Bully Free Classroom (Free Spirit, 1999) is also available in several languages. For more information, visit his website at www. bullyfree.com.

INTRODUCTION

You know firsthand that parenting isn't an easy job. It seems that the job is more complicated today and that parents need more guidance than ever before. It is sadly ironic that we train people in how to fulfill the requirements of almost every job *except* the most important job in the world, parenting. The violence we see in our communities and schools reflects our neglect of providing any guidance for parents. Parents are in grave need of knowledge and skills when it comes to keeping their children safe in neighborhoods and schools.

This book is designed to teach you some of those skills. It is written just for you, the parent, and will help you prevent your child from becoming a victim of bullying. If your child is already being bullied, it will help you stop the mistreatment and help you give your child hope. It is designed to be an informative, practical, and useful tool. The book comprises important information about bullying as well as effective, practical tips and suggestions for you to help your children.

Throughout this book, I repeat certain themes. This is intentional, for I hope that you and your family never forget these themes.

Important Themes

- Everyone must understand the nature and seriousness of bullying.

- Because school violence is a problem of the heart, hearts must be changed.

- We all must value and live the Golden Rule: treat others the way you want to be treated.

- We all need to strive to be peacemakers.

- No one deserves to be mistreated, and we must not tolerate mistreatment.

- To prevent and stop bullying, school personnel, students, parents, and others in the community must work together. Parents and their children play a key role in this effort.

Overview of the Contents

Your first task as a parent is to learn as much as you can about the nature of bullying. If you don't understand the problem, it is more difficult to help your child. Chapter One, "The Nature of Bullying," provides you with such information—defining bullying and describing the types of bullying behaviors that often make up a bullying situation. You will also learn how boys and girls differ in their bullying behavior. Because most bullying occurs in secret, adults often underestimate the problem. Therefore, this chapter also discusses research findings regarding the frequency of bullying and where it is most likely to occur. The last portion of this chapter then presents the rationale for preventing and stopping bullying in all environments.

Chapter Two, "Warning Signs," discusses why children often do not report bullying to their parents or other adults. Because your child may not tell you, it is important for you to know the warning signs that your child is being mistreated or is himself bullying others.

We know that children can be cruel, but we don't often discuss why. Chapter Three, "Possible Causes of Bullying," presents a comprehensive examination of possible causes of bullying. When I developed my anti-bullying program, I spent most of my initial research time identifying these possible causes because I believe it's a key step to finding solutions.

Parenting has it blessings and struggles. The responsibilities are awesome and sometimes overwhelming. All good parents want their children to be able to deal with the challenges associated with new relationships, and their goal is for their children to be caring, sensitive, and resilient. Chapter Four, "Giving Your Child a Good Start," will provide you with some excellent practical and effective strategies for helping children develop into young people and adults who have self-control, healthy self-esteem, and empathy.

No child deserves to be mistreated and rejected. However, sometimes children do need to make some changes in order to increase the likelihood that they will be accepted. Chapter Five, "Promoting Your Child's Acceptance," provides you with an array of strategies to help your child be accepted and have a sense of belonging, while still remaining true to himself and to your values.

When a child is bullied, she sometimes feels helpless and hopeless, and if parents find out their child is being bullied, they sometimes feel helpless as well. What should you do if you find out your child is being bullied? Chapter Six, "Helping Your Bullied Child," answers that question.

Cyberbullying is a growing problem. Children are using computers, cell phones, and other electronic devices and means to mistreat others. Chapter Seven, "Preventing Cyberbullying," describes some important steps to take to prevent your child from being cyberbullied.

Bullies are everywhere. Sometimes children are bullied not only at school but also in their neighborhoods. I have met parents who have considered moving because they could not find an answer to this problem. Chapter Eight, "Neighborhood Bullying," is an exploration of preventive measures you can take if your child is experiencing bullying in your neighborhood.

Older or stronger or even just more popular siblings have an important role to play in helping their brother or sister who is being bullied. Whether at school or in the neighborhood and community, siblings can take steps to stop the bullying. Chapter Nine, "Supportive Tips for Siblings," provides you with tips to share with your child's siblings.

Just as it breaks a parent's heart to see her child being mistreated, so it breaks the heart of good parents who cannot seem to find effective ways stop their children from mistreating others. We should not assume that all parents of children who mistreat others are bad parents who are themselves abusive. Parents of mistreated children need to understand that their children may become bullies, and to take steps to keep that from happening. Chapter Ten, "When Your Child Bullies Others," is a chapter that should not be skipped by parents of mistreated children and is a must-read for parents of children who bully others.

Children can be either victims, bullies, followers, or bystanders. Followers and bystanders have a more important role than you may think in the act of bullying. Followers are those who join in on the bullying or laugh or encourage the bullying in other ways. Followers are not necessarily friends of the bullies. They may be following the bully to avoid becoming targets themselves. Bystanders are children who ignore the mistreatment or who may stand at a distance and laugh. In our anti-bullying program (the Bully Free Program), we seek to empower bystanders. These are usually children who have good hearts and must learn to take a stand against bullying. Chapter Eleven, "When Your Child Is a Bystander," tells you how to empower your child who is a bystander.

Parents need to understand the thoughts and feelings of victims that sometimes drive them to make tragic choices. Chapter Twelve, "Why Some Victims Retaliate, Self-Harm, and/or Commit Suicide," is designed to help you understand the path that some victims take from hurt, to fear, to overwhelming anxiety, to anger, to hate, to rage, and then to retaliation, self-mutilation, and/or suicide.

Unfortunately, not all schools have anti-bullying programs. Some use some anti-bullying materials and resources; others have not yet initiated an effective effort to prevent and stop the problem. Some states have passed laws requiring schools to have at least policies and procedures for dealing with bullying. You can play an important role in encouraging anti-bullying efforts. Chapter Thirteen, "Working with Your Child's School," tells you what to do to encourage your child's school to develop a schoolwide program and how you can support such a program.

Protect Your Child

from

Bullying

1

The Nature of Bullying

Dear Dr. Beane:

I was at the parent presentation you gave several weeks ago for our school system. I was inspired by your knowledge and passion for preventing and stopping bullying. Your son's story broke my heart. I am so afraid for my son. Your son's story sounded a lot like my son's. I have talked several times with his teachers and principal. They don't seem to understand the hurt caused by my son's mistreatment. I wish they were at the parent presentation. When I explain what is happening to my son, they seem to minimize it as normal conflict and say that all children have to learn to deal with conflict. How can I change their thinking? How can I help them see that my son is being destroyed by bullying?

It is important for you to know the difference between bullying and normal conflict. Some types of conflict are a normal part of life. Not all conflict is meant to be hurtful, and coping with such situations can help prepare your child for life in a positive way. Therefore, do not intervene too quickly when you observe conflict between your child and others. However, if you have verified that true bullying is occurring, you should intervene and teach your child skills to stop the bullying. Behavior has exceeded the bounds of normal conflict when

- It is meant to hurt and harm your child.

- It seems intense and has been occurring over a significant period of time.

- The person hurting your child seeks to have power and control over your child.

- No apologies are forthcoming.

- The behavior has a negative impact on your child.

What Is Bullying?

Understanding bullying is an important step in helping your child. When we don't fully understand a problem, we deal only with the symptoms of the problem and not the root causes. After reading this book, you may be more knowledgeable about bullying than the teachers at your child's school. You may be able to provide leadership or at least encouragement to anti-bullying efforts in your child's school. The next few pages are designed to equip you with facts about bullying.

The term *bullying* describes a wide range of behaviors that can have an impact on a person's property, body, feelings, relationships, reputation, and social status. Bullying is a form of overt and aggressive behavior that is intentional, hurtful, and persistent (repeated). Bullied children are teased, harassed, socially rejected, threatened, belittled, and assaulted or attacked (verbally, physically, psychologically) by one or more individuals. There are unequal levels of affect (that is, the victim is upset and distressed while the bully is calm) and often an imbalance of strength (power and dominance).[1] This imbalance of power can be physical or psychological, or your child may simply be outnumbered.

There are times when bullying can be considered violent. All bullying is serious, but when it is intense and lasts for a significant period, it is very serious—it is violent. In fact, bullying is the most common form of school violence. It is violence because it is so destructive to the well-being of children and can lead children to harm themselves and to harm others.

Some of the key words in our definition of bullying are *intentional*, *hurtful*, *persistent*, and *imbalance of strength*. Thus behavior such as teasing that is not intended to hurt and is not persistent is not considered bullying. However, even playful teasing can easily escalate into a bullying situation. Those who have power over the child may repeatedly use the teasing comments to hurt her.

What Does Bullying Look Like?

Bullying behaviors come in a variety of forms: physical, verbal, and social and relational. When it comes to cruelty, children can be incredibly creative. In fact, it would be very difficult to list every possible behavior that makes up a bullying situation. But let's take a look at some of them.

Physical Bullying

Bullying behaviors that are more physical in nature include the following:

- Hitting, slapping, elbowing, and shouldering (slamming)
- Pushing, shoving, and tripping
- Kicking
- Taking or stealing, damaging, or defacing belongings
- Restraining
- Pinching
- Flushing someone's head in the toilet
- Cramming someone into his locker

- Attacking with spit wads, food, and so on
- Threats and body language that are intimidating

It is important not to minimize any of these behaviors. They all can be hurtful, even things that may seem like "horseplay." One nine-year-old boy said, "When they push you in front of your friends and you fall down, it is very embarrassing and humiliating." Restraining someone against her will can also be very hurtful because it is often accompanied by some other inappropriate behavior. For example, one sixteen-year-old girl was held down on the floor by a group of girls who then marked all over her face with a permanent marker. You can imagine how hurt she was emotionally.

Pinching and many other forms of physical bullying are beneath the radar screen of teachers. One teacher told me about an eight-year-old girl who reported at the end of the year that the boy sitting behind her had pinched her back all year long. She had bruises all over her back. The teacher did not know this was happening because the little girl was afraid to tell her.

When I speak to a group of students, it is not unusual for a significant number of students to raise their hands when I ask, "How many of you have had your heads flushed in the toilet?" This is called "swirling." In one school, where the principal told the newspaper that there was no bullying in his school, about one-fourth of the students said they had had their heads flushed. Being crammed into one's locker almost every day is also not uncommon. I have met several students who no longer use their lockers because they know they will be mistreated there. They carry all their books in a backpack.

Verbal Bullying

Verbal bullying can sometimes be more hurtful than physical bullying. Unfortunately, some children learn very quickly that "Sticks and stones may break my bones, but words can hurt me more and for a longer time." The following are some examples of verbal bullying behaviors:

- Name-calling
- Insulting remarks and put-downs
- Repeated teasing
- Racist remarks and harassment
- Threats and intimidation
- Whispering about someone behind her back

Verbal bullying can be very destructive to the well-being of children. When I speak to students, I try to illustrate this point by hitting an apple with my fist. Then I ask, "What is going to happen to this apple?" Of course, they respond, "It's going to be bruised." When you look at the outside of the apple, it doesn't look bruised, but it is. When you call someone a name, it doesn't appear to hurt him, but it bruises him on the inside.

Many times, physical bullying is accompanied by verbal bullying. The following e-mail message from a parent describes this combination.

Dear Dr. Beane:

I have been struggling with my seven-year-old son. He is in second grade at a wonderful school. We are making huge sacrifices for him to attend and hope that our other two children will also attend this school as they get older. In a nutshell, my son had his head slammed against a brick wall and his throat held while these two students were saying, "You had better not tell a lie again about my friend." There have been many instances of verbal bullying over the school year. They

have said things such as, "Shut up, you stupid head,"
and "You are going to get it on the playground!"

Of course, racism is behind a lot of bullying. One seventh-grade boy told me that he had been made fun of ever since second grade, just because of the color of his skin. So when you help schools prevent bullying, you are also helping them combat racism.

Social and Relational Bullying

When most parents think about bullying, they think about mistreatment that is physical and verbal. They do not realize that bullying can also be social and relational. The following are some examples of this form of bullying:

- Destroying and manipulating relationships (for example, turning someone's best friend against her)
- Destroying reputations (gossiping, spreading nasty and malicious rumors and lies about someone)
- Excluding someone from a group (social rejection, isolation)
- Embarrassment and humiliation
- Negative body language, threatening gestures
- Hurtful graffiti or notes passed around
- Cyberbullying (via web pages, e-mail, text messages, and so on)

These kinds of behaviors are prevalent among girls. I had a principal call me one day and tell me about two girls who were excluding others. The principal said she had several girls who went home crying and that their mothers called her because their daughters were so upset. After investigating the problem, the principal discovered that these two girls declared themselves so special that if any other girl wanted to have lunch with them in the cafeteria, she had to sign up and be selected. When I tell this story to groups of students, I am amazed at the number of times I have been told of girls who get a kick out of excluding others, even labeling themselves as the "Royal Five" or some other name.

Exclusion is even seen in preschool children. They often will not let others play with them and encourage others not to play with someone.

Much of girl bullying seems to stem from jealousy, which leads to anger and then to efforts to destroy someone's relationships or reputation. An example of such behavior is described in the following e-mail message.

Dear Dr. Beane,

I'm sure you get e-mails all the time, but I hope you have the time to help me with a problem. My daughter, Brook, is a new student in a fairly small high school. She is very attractive and outgoing. In fact, I don't think she has ever met a stranger. Brook seems to draw people to her. Of course, the boys at the new school got very interested in her, especially this one boy. He has a girlfriend, but he always wants to hang around and talk to Brook. Of course, his girlfriend is jealous and is now spreading rumors that my daughter is a whore and has had several nervous breakdowns. I hear my daughter crying in her bed at night. My heart aches for her. I don't know what to do. She won't let me call the girl's parents and she doesn't want me to talk to the school about it.

Why Do Children Bully?

Children bully others for a variety of reasons. Sometimes they are impulsive and mistreat others without thinking about their actions or the consequences. They often want to dominate others, exercising power and control over them in order to hurt them. They like feeling big in front of their peers. This power seems to net them some social status. However, they may continuously seek to prove their status. They may have more family problems than normal and take out their frustration and anger on others. To do this, they pick on students who they view as weaker than they, exhibiting little or no sympathy for victims.

Some bullies mistreat others because they are experiencing or observing abuse in the home or have not been disciplined appropriately at a young age. Their parents may have also failed to teach them the importance of respect, sensitivity, empathy, and kindness. There are a host of other possible causes of bullying, which I address in Chapter Three.

Are There Different Types of Bullies?

According to Olweus, there are three different types of bullies: the aggressive bully, the passive bully, and the bully-victim.[2] Aggressive bullies tend to be physically strong, impulsive, hot tempered, belligerent, fearless, coercive, confident, and lacking in empathy. Passive bullies tend to be insecure, and they are much less popular than aggressive bullies. They sometimes have low self-esteem, have few likable qualities, and often have unhappy home lives. The bully-victims represent a small percentage of bullies. These are children who have experienced bullying themselves, whether at home or at school. They are typically physically weaker than the bullies at school, but stronger than those they bully.

Dieter Wolke of the University of Hertfordshire, England, identified a fourth group of bullies: pure bullies.[3] They appear to be healthy individuals who enjoy school. They use bullying to obtain dominance. Pure bullies just seem to enjoy bullying others.

Are There Different Types of Victims?

According to Olweus, there are three types of victims: passive victims, provocative victims, and bully-victims, which we discussed earlier.[4] Passive victims represent the largest group of victims. They do not directly provoke bullies; they appear to be physically weaker students and do not defend themselves. Passive victims also appear to have few, if any, friends. Sometimes they are children who have been overprotected by their parents. Some researchers have identified subgroups of this group of victims.[5] For example, vicarious victims are students who are affected by the fear and anxiety created by a school culture that allows bullying. They are fearful they may become victims. False victims are a small group of students who complain frequently and without justification to teachers about being bullied. Perpetual victims are individuals who are bullied all their lives and may even develop a victim mentality.[6]

Provocative victims represent a smaller group than the passive victims. They can actually be aggressive themselves, especially toward others who appear weaker than they are. Because they may have poor anger management skills, their peers may not like them. They often react negatively to conflict or losing.

How Are Girls and Boys Different in Their Bullying Behavior?

Both boys and girls engage in physical, verbal, and social bullying. Because the behavior of boys has been more observable, we have thought boys bully more than girls, but now most experts aren't sure that this is true. We often underestimate girl bullying, as girls can be sneaky, and their bullying behavior is more frequently social and relational.

Typically, boys use more physical aggression than girls. However, it appears that girls are becoming more physical. Perhaps they are watching more television shows that teach them that it is okay to be physically violent and to attack males. The following are some typical characteristics of girl bullies and boy bullies.

Girl bullies

- Are more likely to bully other girls—but may bully some boys
- Engage in group bullying more than boys
- Seek to inflict psychological pain on their victims
- Can appear to be angels around adults while being cruel to peers
- Frequently make comments regarding the sexual behavior of girls they don't like
- Attack within a tightly knit networks of friends

Boy bullies

- Are more physical (tripping, spitting, quick blows, pushing, and so on)
- Use verbal attacks regarding sexual orientation and family members
- Tend to attack physically smaller and weaker individuals
- Engage in sexual harassment
- Engage in extortion

How Frequently Does Bullying Occur?

Because bullying occurs most often in secret, away from the eyes of adults, parents and school personnel often underestimate bullying. Therefore, they sometimes don't understand the intensity of the problem or the need to implement a schoolwide anti-bullying program.

Worldwide prevalence rates of bullying of students range from 10 percent of secondary students to 27 percent of middle school students. According to the World Health Organization, the prevalence of bullying is quite consistent across countries.[7] Bullying is so prevalent that it is a constant hum in our schools and in some neighborhoods. It is estimated that 30 percent of teens in the United States (over 5.7 million) are involved in bullying as a bully, a target of bullying, or both.[8] A study of fifteen thousand U.S. students in grades 6–10 found that 17 percent of students reported having been bullied "sometimes or more often" during the school year. Approximately 19 percent said they bullied others "sometimes or more often," and 6 percent reported both bullying and being a victim of bullying. Some researchers state that 20 to 25 percent of schoolchildren are bullied. Six out of ten American students witness bullying at least once a day.[9]

Now that you understand that bullying is a frequent occurrence, it is important for you to know when and where it is most likely to happen to your child. Even though the majority of bullying is done in secret, there are some typical high-risk areas and high-risk times.

When and Where Does Bullying Occur?

Unfortunately, bullying happens almost everywhere. It happens in homes, in neighborhoods and communities, and in workplaces. We know that bullying often starts in the preschool years (around age three) and increases in frequency and becomes more physical toward the end of the elementary years. Bullying peaks during the middle school years and is often in its cruelest form during those years.[10] It decreases in high school, but can still be very hurtful. The physical severity of bullying may decrease with the bully's age.[11]

At the beginning of each school year, bullies go "shopping" for easy targets, victims they can hurt and over whom they can have physical or psychological power. This is why it is important for your child to tell a trusted adult right away if he is being bullied. Also teach your child how to look confident and to hide the fact that what a bully does or says hurts him. There are several tips in this book to help your child communicate that he is not an easy target.

Bullying occurs while children travel to and from school, but it is more likely to happen on school property. Bullying seems to happen everywhere, but the typical high-risk areas are places where there is no adult supervision, inadequate adult supervision, or lack of structure—areas where children have nothing to do or are free to do as they wish. Some of the school-related high-risk areas are buses, bus stops, bathrooms, hallways, cafeterias, playgrounds, locker rooms, gyms, parking lots, stairwells, between buildings, and even classrooms. Therefore, you should encourage your child's school to improve supervision, in terms not only of the number of adults but also of the quality of supervision they provide. They should be trained to supervise their areas, and schools should be encouraged to add structure to unstructured times.

When I work with schools, I suggest strategies that include the following:

- Increase adult supervision by using trained volunteers.

- Require and train school personnel to supervise high-risk areas.

- Assign seats in the cafeteria and rotate the assignments so that children are always sitting with other children their own age.

- Require students to engage in activities that include everyone prior to going to recess.

- Require assigned seats on the bus (that is, high school students in the rear, elementary school students in the middle, and middle school students toward the front).

- Require students to stand in designated areas by grade while waiting for school to start.

- Enforce behavioral expectations and rules for all the high-risk areas.

Why Must Bullying Be Prevented and Stopped?

Your response to this question is, of course, "Because it hurts my child." That is certainly reason enough, but there are more reasons. Bullied children are often so persistently mistreated that they do not have time to recover from the previous experiences. Bullying can thus have consequences that go well beyond individual incidents. It is not surprising to see children trying to "fly away" from the mistreatment, which can lead them to make destructive choices and sometimes creates more problems. Bullying is connected to many other problems that could touch the life of your child and others.

When a child is bullied, he may be afraid to go to school. He may get sick on Sunday night and nauseated on Monday morning just thinking about going to school and facing the bullies. Each day is a social minefield with several unknown, potentially dangerous events in the day's path. The fear, anxiety, and stress may cause your child to pretend to be sick, skip school, or skip classes. According to the American Medical Association, about 160,000 students a day stay home because of bullying.[12] In addition to causing students to fall behind in their schoolwork, these debilitating emotions can lead to a sense of helplessness and depression—even posttraumatic stress. For some children, bullying is very traumatic; it may be traumatic for your child.

Fear, anxiety, and stress are closely followed by anger and helplessness—perhaps even hopelessness. This is a toxic mix of emotions that may create toxic shame. This is poisonous shame that can cause your child to question his ability to cope with the bullying. He may also question whether he can trust the adults around him to help him. Your child may come to feel that he deserves to be bullied because he is defective in some way. He may feel additional shame because he cannot "stand up for himself" as you have taught him to do. If this shame and the accompanying misconceptions are not dealt with, your child could feel that he cannot trust life (especially school life) to be good to him anymore. This does not have to be the path your child takes. You can help him, and so can professional counseling.

TOXIC SHAME

Toxic shame can cause your child to harm himself (self-mutilate) and/or even to commit suicide. I have met several students who cut themselves. They tell me they cut themselves in order to release the hurt caused by bullying or to cause a physical pain that may minimize the pain in their hearts. If your child is being victimized, I encourage you to examine your child's body each night as he steps out of the tub or shower. Sometimes children cut themselves where their clothes will hide the cuts, but sometimes you can see scars between their knuckles or on their wrists. Make sure if you do find evidence of self-mutilation that you get your child professional help.

Children who are persistently mistreated and experience depression for a significant amount of time may have suicidal thoughts. Any talk about suicide is serious and needs immediate attention. Watch for signs that your child is at risk of committing suicide. (If you have observed some of the warning signs of suicide risk, please refer to Chapter Six for a list of signs and a list of questions to ask your child.) If your child talks about committing suicide, do not assume he does not mean it. If you suspect your child is suicidal, seek professional help and do not leave him alone.

Bullying also can lead a child to join a gang, cult, hate group, or drug group. Every child feels an intense need to belong and to be accepted by some group. When this need cannot be satisfied through typical peer relationships, your child may seek to belong to a destructive and possibly dangerous group of individuals.

Bullying is also a common theme in the majority of school shootings. After years of mistreatment, some victims of bullying travel a very sad and dangerous path from hurt to revenge. (See Chapter Twelve for more on why some victims retaliate.)

KEY MESSAGES

- Behavior that is meant to hurt and harm your child should not be considered normal conflict.

- The term *bullying* describes a wide range of behaviors that can impact a person's property, body, feelings, relationships, reputation, and social status.

- All forms of bullying can be destructive to the well-being of children and can create unsafe homes, neighborhoods, and schools.

- Both girls and boys can be physical, verbal, and social and relational in their bullying. Girls tend to do more social and relational bullying.

- Bullying occurs to some degree in every school.

- Adults often underestimate the prevalence of the problem.

- Bullying happens everywhere, especially where there is a lack of supervision or lack of structure. Some of the high-risk areas are bathrooms, hallways, stairwells, cafeterias, locker rooms, parking lots, buses, common areas, bus stops, and classrooms.

- Bullying can create toxic shame and cause children to be sick, to hurt themselves, and even to commit suicide.

- Bullying can lead students to form or join gangs, hate groups, and cults.

- Bullying is a common theme of most school shootings.

2

Warning Signs

Dear Dr. Beane:

As you spoke at the conference, I could feel my blood pressuring rising. When you discussed the characteristics of a victim, my heart sank. I could not believe the number of warning signs that described my child. As you spoke, I became convinced he is a victim of bullying. You may not remember, but I left the ballroom before you ended your speech. I had to go call my wife and tell her that we really needed to talk to our son. Thank you for opening my eyes and for making it possible for us to help our son.

Bullying takes children places psychologically and physically they should never have to go, and as I discussed in Chapter One, it is connected to many other problems (depression, drugs, alcohol, gangs, cults, and so on). Unfortunately, children often do not tell adults, not even their parents, that they are being bullied or that others are being bullied. This chapter discusses why children will not tell adults about bullying and lists warning signs that might indicate that your child is persistently being mistreated.

Why Don't Children Tell Their Parents or Other Adults?

There are several reasons your child may not tell you that she is being mistreated. For one, children are taught very early not to be a "tattletale" or to "rat" on their peers. They think that telling someone they are being hurt or that someone else is being hurt is wrong. When your child expresses this concern, explain that when she tattles on someone, she is trying to get that person into trouble. In contrast, when she reports mistreatment, she is trying to help someone, not get a person into trouble. She is doing what a good human being should do. So tell her you expect her to "report" when she is mistreated and when other children are mistreated.

Another reason children will not tell an adult is that they have experienced adults' doing nothing about reported bullying. Some children have told me that they have observed adults ignoring obvious mistreatment, and have reported that their teachers have even said, "Don't bother me," gesturing that they want to be left alone. Unfortunately, there are some teachers who do not want to get involved because they are afraid it could mean a lot of extra work for them as well as meetings with the parents. Some teachers and administrators also feel that they need to stay focused on academics and leave social issues to others. What these teachers don't understand is that bullying has a negative impact on learning and school performance.

Some children do not tell adults because they are afraid that adult involvement may make the situation worse. This fear is sometimes justified. For example, sometimes when a parent of a victim calls the bully's parents, the bully teases the victim: "Your mother called my mother last night. You big baby." Another example is when the child tells a teacher at school and the teacher only halfheartedly warns the bully—almost in a joking manner—because he believes that the victim is weak. Sensing indirect support from the adult, the bully steps up the mistreatment. This is why school personnel need to be trained to investigate rumors and unverified reports of bullying and to respond appropriately when bullying behavior is observed.

Some students are embarrassed or ashamed to tell adults because they've come to believe that the bullying is their fault—that there is something wrong with them or that they were incapable of stopping it on their own. Other children will not tell their parents because they do not want them to worry about them. When I speak to students, parents, and teachers, I tell my son's story. He told us initially about the mistreatment, but as it persisted he hid it from us. I feel that he did not tell us because he loved us too much—he did not want us to worry about him. I tell children not to love their parents too much. It is their parents' job to worry about them. It is their parents' right to know what they are thinking, feeling, and experiencing.

What Are the Warning Signs That Your Child Is a Victim of Bullying?

Review the warning signs in the following list. When you see your child exhibiting any of these warning signs, you need to pay attention to what is happening in your child's life, get closer to your child, and be ready to step up your involvement. Keep in mind that some of these signs may be evident even if your child is not being bullied. If you see a number of these signs over time, however, you should suspect that your child is a victim of bullying and take steps to protect her immediately.

Warning Signs of Bullying

- Has difficulty concentrating in class and is easily distracted
- Wants to take a different route to school or different transportation to school
- Has a sudden lack of interest in school-sponsored activities and events
- Has a sudden drop in grades
- Seems happy on weekends, but unhappy and preoccupied or tense on Sundays

- Uses "victim" body language—hunches shoulders, hangs head, won't look people in the eye, and backs off from others
- Suddenly prefers the company of adults
- Has frequent illnesses (headaches, stomachaches, pains) or fakes illness
- Suffers from fatigue
- Has nightmares and insomnia
- Comes home with unexplainable scratches and bruises
- Suddenly develops a stammer or stutter
- Has a change in eating patterns
- Seems overly concerned about personal safety; spends a lot of time and effort thinking or worrying about getting safely to and from school and getting around in the school (to and from lunch, to and from recess, to and from the bathroom, to and from the lockers, and so on)
- Talks about avoiding certain areas of the school
- Carries protection devices, such as a knife, box opener, fork, or gun (see Chapter Four for a discussion of weapons)
- Frequently asks for extra money (supposedly for lunch, school supplies, and the like)
- Possessions are often "lost," damaged, or destroyed without an explanation
- Has a sudden change in behavior (bed-wetting, nail-biting, tics, and so on)
- Cries easily or often, becomes emotionally distraught, and has extreme mood swings
- Cries herself to sleep
- Blames herself for problems and difficulties

- Consistently talks about being made fun of, laughed at, picked on, teased, put down, or pushed around
- Talks about being threatened, kicked, hit, or otherwise physically attacked (deserving your immediate attention)
- Talks about students telling lies about her, gossiping about her, or excluding her from a group
- Talks about not being able to stand up for herself
- Talks about dropping out of school
- Suddenly starts bullying other students or siblings
- Becomes overly aggressive, rebellious, and unreasonable
- Has a sudden loss of respect for authority figures
- Seeks the wrong friends in the wrong places
- Talks about forming or joining a cult or other suspicious group
- Has a sudden interest in violent movies, video games, and books
- Talks about running away
- Talks about feeling depressed
- Talks about or attempts suicide

Perhaps as you read this list, your heart was struck with fear. That is a normal response of any good parent. The good news is that there is much you can do. In the next chapter, I discuss what you should do before any of the warning signs occur and what you can do when they do occur.

KEY MESSAGES

- Children often do not tell adults that they or someone else is being bullied. There are several reasons why: they are afraid the adults will do nothing or even make it worse; they don't want to be a "tattletale" or to "rat" on someone; they are embarrassed or feel shame; they don't want their parents to worry about them.

- Some warning signs that your child may be a victim of bullying are a sudden lack of interest in school-sponsored activities, a drop in school grades, a preference for the company of adults, nightmares and trouble sleeping, anger and irritability, unexplained physical injuries, avoidance of school, depression and anxiety.

- Presence of any of the warning signs doesn't necessarily mean that your child is being bullied, but they mean you should pay close attention to your child's behavior, especially if several of the warning signs are present.

3

Possible Causes of Bullying

Dear Dr. Beane:

My son is in third grade and has cried every morning, not wanting to go to school. We have tried everything we know to do to get him to go to school. We have pleaded with him to tell us why he doesn't want to go to school. After several weeks, he finally told us that a boy bullies him at school. He pushes my son, he throws things at him and yesterday my son came home with a big bruise on his arm. He has asked, "Why are they being mean to me, Mom?" We don't know what to tell him. Why are some children cruel to others?

Understanding why some children are cruel to others and why some are singled out as victims can help us develop a variety of solutions and strategies to address all the possible causes. It also improves our ability to discuss bullying with children. We can help them understand how their behavior has been shaped by their families, surroundings, and even the way they spend their leisure time. Both bullies and victims are products of our society and are reflections of the quality of our families, schools, and communities. Both are victims and children at risk, and they both need help. Some of the numerous factors that *may* contribute to bullying are discussed in this chapter.

Physical Influences

Innate Preferences

Research indicates that humans may be born with a preference for certain physical characteristics in individuals.[1] Tom Cash, a psychologist at Old Dominion University who has studied the effect of individuals' appearance on observers for more than twenty years, says that when babies are shown pictures of two faces, one considered more attractive than the other by a majority of adults, they look longer at the more attractive faces. Infants at the age of three months also respond to "pretty" faces. Infants at twelve months show withdrawal and aversive reactions to "homelier" faces. If humans have an innate preference for more "attractive" people, they are more likely to treat the "unattractive" in a less favorable manner. This is called *lookism.*

Adults also have these same preferences. In fact, they are surprisingly consistent in their descriptions of the features of attractive individuals: big eyes, high cheekbones, and a narrow jaw. Their descriptions are consistent regardless of the race or cultural background of the adults.

Studies show that our perception of beauty may be hard-wired in our brains. In studies conducted at Massachusetts General Hospital, Harvard Medical School, and Massachusetts Institute of Technology, researchers Itzhak Aharon, Nancy Etcoff, Dan Ariely, Christopher F. Chabris, Ethan O'Connor, and Hans C. Breiter have used magnetic resonance imaging (MRI) technology to look at the activity in men's brains when they were shown pictures of beautiful women's faces. Breiter and his colleagues found that the same part of the brain lights up as when a hungry person sees food, or a gambler eyes cash, or a drug addict sees a fix. Essentially, beauty and addiction trigger the same areas in the brain.[2] But just because our perception of good looks is hard-wired, this does not mean we cannot control our interactions with others.

Biological Factors

Some experts believe that aggression is a basic, inherent human characteristic, but certain biological factors may increase the level of aggression beyond acceptable norms. For example, high levels of endogenous testosterone seem to encourage aggressive behavior in men designed to inflict harm on another person, but can also take the form of antisocial behavior.[3] For example, higher levels of testosterone have been found even in some preschool bullies.

A University of Michigan study conducted by Michelle Wirth and Oliver Schultheiss[4] has identified another possible cause of bullying. It appears that the human brain may have a built-in mechanism that detects and responds to emotions perceived in the faces of others. The responses of people to the perceived emotions vary. For example, participants in the study with high levels of testosterone seemed to enjoy or be rewarded by an annoyed look or angry face caused by mistreatment. This seems to occur on a nonconscious level. Therefore, bullies feel rewarded for mistreating others.

Temperament

It is well documented that a child's temperament is a significant contributing factor to bullying.[5] Temperament can be defined as the mixture of elements or qualities that make up an individual's personality. These permanently affect the way a person acts, feels, and thinks. For example, a child with a "hotheaded" temperament, who is active and impulsive, is more inclined to be aggressive with other children than a child who has a calm temperament.

Social Influences

Because humans are social, relational creatures, we influence others and are influenced by others. Parents can be very powerful teachers. They can have either a positive or negative impact on their children. The media and peers are also very powerful teachers. Therefore, good parents are in a constant battle with the negative influences of this world. Unfortunately some parents are not good influences and teach preferences, biases, and values that promote conflict and other relational problems.

Learned Preferences

In addition to their innate preferences, children also learn preferences from their families and from society. Children are taught very early to value appearance, intelligence, strength, power, influence, persistence, and productivity. They learn what is within the range of "normal" at a very early age, and they constantly shape and redefine their *acceptance range*.

Belief in One's Own Superiority

Children are sometimes taught that they are better than others and not to associate with children who are perceived as "losers" or to worry too much about those children's struggles. The prevailing attitude in our culture is to be special, look better, achieve more, be on top, be number one, and be the best, no matter what it takes. Such thinking causes some people to play the "game" of looking for reasons they are superior to others. Playing such a game includes comparing oneself to those one considers inferior. The media have supported this kind of thinking by promoting the stereotypes of winners who have it all, versus losers who deserve only our scorn. If someone does not perform, he tends to be pushed to the side.

Violence, Aggression, and Conflict in the Media

The media have a tremendous impact on children today. Some research indicates that children who view a lot of violence on television, in videos, in video games, and in movies often become more aggressive and less empathic toward others. In fact, the consensus among researchers on television violence is that there is a measurable increase from 3 to 15 percent in an individual's aggressive behavior after watching violent television.[6] Children tend to emulate what they are exposed to. Some of the popular reality television shows and even news talk shows have promoted and even glamorized conflict. Many of these shows provide a continuous stream of put-downs, cruel comments, and rejection.

Television and movie violence can be harmful to young children. Although there is controversy regarding the effect of media violence on children, there is sufficient research to support the belief that such violence can cause children to become frightened, worried, suspicious, and aggressive. In a study conducted by the Kaiser Family Foundation in 2003, nearly half (47 percent) of parents with children between the ages of four and six reported that their children have imitated aggressive behaviors they saw on television.[7] This has not been fully explained, but it should encourage parents to exert more control over what their children watch and how much they watch. Unfortunately, the amount of violence on television is increasing. Even cartoons are becoming more and more violent. And because television is often used as a babysitter, children at a very young age are viewing aggression and violence toward others as acceptable behavior. Research conducted by the University of Washington in Seattle found that the more television four-year-olds watched, the more likely they were to mistreat others by the time they were eleven years old.[8] Of course, supervised viewing of television can have a positive impact on kids. The Kaiser Family Foundation also found that 87 percent of kids mimic positive behaviors observed on television.[9]

Many video games encourage or require children to be actively involved in violent actions. There has been a steady increase in the number of video games with violent themes.

As I have reviewed the history of victims of bullying who have retaliated, I have noticed that many of them engaged in violent video games. Such games gave them a psychological release from the anger and hurt they experienced from bullying. Walt Mueller, president of the Center for Parent/Youth Understanding, says that it appears that children are using fantasy games as outlets for real-life anger and aggression.[10] Such games allow the victim to retaliate in a more acceptable manner. When a victim is thinking about retaliation, the violent video games could give him ideas for carrying out his revenge. They may also provide some means of retaliation practice, something of a murder simulator. It is important to remember that regardless of the effect of violent video games, the root of the problem is bullying—how children are treating each other.

David Walsh, a child psychologist who has coauthored a study connecting violent video games to physical aggression, has identified a possible link between underdeveloped impulse control and violent video games. He says the link can be explained in part by pioneering brain research recently done at the National Institutes of Health. The impulse control center of the brain—the part of the brain that enables us to think ahead, consider consequences, and manage urges—is the part of the brain right behind our forehead called the prefrontal cortex. This part of the brain is "under construction" during the teenage years; its wiring is not completed until an individual is in his early twenties. Walsh says that the development of impulse control can be further hindered in a person who has additional risk factors for criminal behavior.[11] Violence is complex, and there are many contributing factors. Not every child playing violent video games is going to retaliate or engage in violence, because not every child has other risk factors that sometimes interact to bring about violence.

Even music lyrics are becoming increasingly violent. Consider this: 99.2 percent of teenagers (defined as ages twelve to seventeen) listen to radio every week—a higher percentage than for any other age group—and 80.6 percent listen to radio every day.[12] Over the course of a week, the average teenager will listen to 13.5 hours of radio.[13] Music is also used by hate groups to reach youth. Their messages can be repeated over and over in songs several times a day on the radio and on CD players. In 2003, researchers Craig Anderson, Brad Bushman, and Janie Eubanks reported that violent music lyrics increased aggressive thoughts and hostile feelings. They state that there are now good theoretical and empirical reasons to expect the effects of music lyrics on aggressive behavior to be similar to the well-studied effects of exposure to TV and movie violence and to those found in the more recent research efforts on violent video games.[14]

Sports Violence

Sports violence can be defined as behavior that causes harm, occurs outside the rules of the sport, and is unrelated to the competitive objectives of the sport. There has been an increase in the frequency and seriousness of sports violence.[15] The most violent team sports are ice hockey, football, and rugby. Unfortunately, the media sometimes glamorize players who are the most violent, controversial, and aggressive. Children often select these sports heroes as role models and imitate their behavior.

The atmosphere of any sports team is influenced by the adults in charge. The majority of coaches are excellent mentors and role models. Unfortunately, there are some who create an overly aggressive atmosphere and de-emphasize fun, skill development, team building, and social development. Some coaches contribute to bullying through aggressive and unrealistic desires to win at all costs.[16] Such coaches often publicly criticize and humiliate their players with inappropriate language, and may even punish them by giving them less playing time or encouraging other team members to tease and harass them. Many of these adults target not only their players but also other coaches and referees. Unfortunately, even parents are sometimes poor models of sportsmanship and respect at sporting events.

Prejudice

One of the most obvious causes of bullying is prejudice. A prejudice is an attitude we have toward a specific situation or toward a group of people, an attitude we have adopted without sufficient consideration of the facts about the situation or group.[17] People who are prejudiced make judgments about others on unfounded beliefs and fears. Any human difference—in appearance, behavior, or language—can trigger unfounded fears in the prejudiced mind. Such fears keep prejudiced people from acting responsibly as they interact with others and can lead to bullying.

Prejudice begins early in life, grows in ignorance, and will persist if not challenged. Children are the most vulnerable to the harm created by prejudice. According to Doris Sanford, by the time children are five years old, they begin to hear negative opinions from others about their racial heritage and religion.[18] These opinions can be found in their communities and in some television programs adults let them watch. Even with the current emphasis on cultural diversity and political correctness, children are still rejected because of their ethnic, cultural, and religious backgrounds.

Prejudiced children may decide they do not like black students, overweight students, students with disabilities, or students of different nationalities who speak English with difficulty, and will tease, harass, and reject them. They have formed an attitude without knowing the facts.

According to Sanford, black children are more likely to be blamed by peers and adults for wrongdoing than white children in the same classroom.[19] These prejudicial and rejecting behaviors damage the self-image of children and hinder their efforts to be accepted.

Unfortunately, many culturally different individuals and groups face alienation on a daily basis in our schools. I have met several students who say they are bullied because they are religious and do their best to stick to their standards. They are teased, isolated, and verbally and physically abused by their peers because of their refusal to engage in activities that are against their beliefs and desired lifestyles. One student in Florida was teased and harassed so much for dressing according to her religious beliefs that she committed suicide.

Children living in poverty are often targets of bullying in some school settings. The social, economic, and educational exclusion associated with poverty is worsened by bullying, harassment, and discrimination.

Jealousy

A powerful motivator for bullying, especially among girls, is jealousy. For example, a girl who is attractive and popular with boys can anger other girls. These girls can become so jealous that they try to hurt the popular girl. Children often attack those who seem to be perceived as better than average: too attractive, too wealthy, too popular, and so on. In response to this jealous bullying, children can develop a fear of success because they are very aware that success can threaten their acceptance and bring negative consequences (the animosity of classmates, the pressure of others' expectations). Girls may have a significantly greater fear of success than boys. Parents of intelligent and gifted children are also concerned about the acceptance of their children. In fact, they can be so fearful that they may even reject special attention and programs designed to enhance their child's abilities.

Sometimes teachers inadvertently bring on jealousy by singling out a child to do something for them or by praising some children more than others. Children are very sensitive to this favoritism. Some children become jealous and start mistreating the "teacher's pet."

Protecting One's Image

Our self-esteem can be influenced by the degree of perceived similarity between us and those with whom we interact. Therefore, some children may seek to protect their self-image by restricting their range of contacts with people dissimilar (or perceived to be dissimilar) to themselves. Befriending or defending a victim of bullying may be seen as risky to one's reputation. In fact, some children report that they are made fun of for being friends with those who are mistreated. Children often prefer the company of popular children, not because they like them, but because they wish to be identified with those who appear to be popular. Therefore, they may avoid individuals with "negative" attributes. This is most true during the middle school years.

Fear

Fear of being laughed at. All humans are afraid others will laugh at them. As a defense, they may initiate the teasing of others or be willing to join in the teasing and rejection.

Fear of losing what one has. If children are already considered to be members of a popular group, they will be very reluctant to risk their membership by refusing to participate in the rejection of others.

Fear of rejection. Children may fear they will be rejected and, therefore, reject others first to avoid the hurt. Such fear may also encourage other children to join in the rejection. They would rather be rejecting than rejected.

Fear of the unknown. Because people fear the unknown, they tend to associate with individuals who are similar to themselves in terms of nationality, religion, economic class, and so on. This is often called the "birds of a feather syndrome." To avoid interacting with the unknown, some children reject individuals who are considered different. Avoiding or putting down those who are different makes these children feel safer.

Fear of exposure. All humans are afraid that their weaknesses or perceived weaknesses will be exposed to their peers. To avoid revealing their own weaknesses, children who bully may initiate or encourage efforts to expose the weaknesses of others. Some children, for example, avoid exposing their weaknesses by engaging in inappropriate behavior, such as showing disrespect to the teacher.

Self-Centeredness, Lack of Sensitivity, and Desire for Attention

Young children are naturally egocentric and only gradually learn to "de-center." Some children are not taught to be tolerant, sensitive, and appreciative of differences in others. Some are simply spoiled; they have always gotten their way and enjoy experiencing the associated feeling of power and pleasure. Self-centered children have a difficult time understanding how their actions affect others. It is difficult to imagine, but bullies are sometimes unaware of the hurt they cause. They are focused entirely on their own need for power and entertainment.

Sometimes children bully because they want to be the center of attention. This desire for attention can also encourage children to bully others "for the laughs." When these students are confronted privately about their degrading comments, they say something like, "We were just messing around. We didn't realize he was going to get so upset."

Revenge

People who hurt others have often been hurt themselves at some point in their own lives. They may have been mistreated at home by parents or siblings (or both) or by peers in the neighborhood or at school. Some of the bullies I have worked with have a *victim mentality*. They are angry because certain needs have not been met, and they think everyone has misunderstood and will continue to misunderstand them and disrespect them. As a result of their anger and flawed thinking, they strike out at others. They often feel inadequate and compelled to control others, and are unwilling to listen to comments about their inappropriate behavior or to examine their own motives. They may seek to mistreat others as revenge for their own mistreatment. Their thinking is similar to victims who expect to be mistreated, but they act like bullies.

Students who fail to gain recognition through the exercise of power may seek revenge on those who make them feel powerless. They think that hurting others will make up for being hurt themselves or feeling rejected and unloved. Often students who seek revenge don't care about being punished. Instead, being punished may give them a renewed cause for action, reinforcing their sense of victimization. The more trouble they cause for themselves, the more justified they feel in hurting others.

Group Mentality

Children may be rejected, not because of their own behavior or characteristics, but because peer groups need a target for rejection. Such rejection helps the group define the boundaries of their acceptance and bring unity to the group. In other words, the targeted individuals serve as scapegoats for the benefit of group cohesiveness. This is one reason students are so eager to join a clique, even when they do not like the people in it. Their need to feel united with peers is a powerful motive.

One of the rules for belonging to a clique or gang is that you must do as the group does, which may include mistreating others, even members who want to join the group. The practice of hazing, for example, is a group's effort to unite and feel powerful, often by hurting or humiliating new members. Street gangs often have initiation rules that require new members to hurt those in rival gangs. Although the members as individuals may not want to hurt others, they feel that they must in order to remain in the group. Their reward is the safety, power, and respect that being a part of the group represents.

Poor Family Environment

The elements of a home environment that can increase the likelihood that a child will be bullied may also increase the likelihood that the child will bully others. According to Olweus, these home environments have the following traits:[20]

- Lack of warmth and involvement
- Failure to set clear limits to aggressive behavior toward peers, siblings, and adults
- Too little love and care and too much freedom
- Use of power-assertive child-rearing methods—physical punishment and violent emotional outbursts

Whether they want to be or not, parents are the first role models of their children. Parents who express anger physically will likely produce children who tend to express anger physically. Violence begets violence. Fortunately, children who have learned to bully can unlearn the behavior.

Never Being Told Not to Bully

The truth is that some children have never been told not to bully. The parents may be too permissive and allow their children to get away with bullying, or they may not have specifically tried to develop empathy, manners, kindness, and other important character traits in their children.

Poor Self-Esteem

There is considerable debate among researchers regarding the self-concept and self-esteem of bullies. Dan Olweus, a researcher in Norway, has probably done more research than anyone on bullying, and does not believe there is any justification for the opinion that bullies are anxious and insecure. He believes that they have a "relatively positive view of themselves."[21] Ken Rigby, another respected researcher, agrees. He says that bullies have average self-esteem.[22] Some researchers state that bullies may have feelings of inadequacy and displace their feelings onto children who are more vulnerable. Some researchers have discovered that bullies who have not been victims have self-esteem equal to students who are not bullies and who are not victims; in contrast, bullies who have been victims had poor self-esteem.[23] When seeking to help bullies change, we must explore all possibilities. We must carefully examine the self-esteem of the individual bully.

Reaction to Tension

Schools and homes can be filled with tension created by high academic demands. The achievement bar is constantly being raised, and schools are being held accountable for the performance of students. In fact, they may be punished if the students do not meet expectations, causing an increasingly tense atmosphere in schools. Also, increasingly difficult academic content is being taught to younger children. High expectations can improve learning. However, students face more and more accountability examinations that determine their future, and these exams can cause a lot of stress among students. This problem is compounded if parents are not capable of assisting their children with homework and preparation for tests. The resulting tension makes it difficult to have a normal home life. Tension thus permeates the school during the day and the home at night and may be expressed through inappropriate behavior such as bullying.

Seeing Aggression Allowed and Rewarded

A school can be caring and supportive while having zero tolerance for bullying, or it can support bullying by ignoring the problem. Research indicates that many times very little or nothing is done to stop bullying in schools, even when children tell adults about their situation. In fact, there have been times when the reactions of adults have discouraged the bullied and encouraged the bulliers. Children have told me about times when a teacher said, "Don't bother me. You need to learn how to deal with this yourself." One mother told me about an incident in which a student who committed suicide left a note listing the names of those who mistreated him, and the school did nothing to punish their behavior.

Children who bully do get a lot of attention from their peers, so other children see that they have power and are respected for their power. Bullies feel rewarded. They can also seem to be popular because others are afraid of not acting as if they like them.

Children also see aggression being allowed and even rewarded in the media and possibly at home as well. Children who watch wealthy relatives or wealthy television figures bully others are learning that bullies make more money. Children who see a parent who allows herself to be bullied are learning that it's even okay to bully someone you care about.

Desire for Control and Power

For some bullies, the motivation seems to be domination and power. Children are often bullied by stronger and older individuals. Bullies are usually stronger than average, and their victims are usually physically weaker than average. However, bullies can be younger and smaller than their victims. Sometimes they have psychological power over bigger, kinder, and more sensitive students. Small bullies are able to project themselves as "big people." They project such an image by holding their heads, shoulders, and fists high and by using intimidating voices.

Children who bully others for power seem to have little empathy for their victims.

Poor Neighborhood and Community Values

Children who are surrounded by people with good morals are less likely to be bullies. For example, psychologists and professional mental health professionals have found that supportive religion can make a big difference in the lives of children, especially adolescents. Andrew Weaver found that teenagers who are involved in religious institutions (1) are less likely to attempt suicide and less likely to think about doing so, (2) report less depression and are less likely to experience depression that is at a clinically significant level when they are depressed, (3) are less likely to favor casual sex and more likely to wait longer before they become sexually active, (4) are more likely to find meaning in traumatic events and experience lower distress and faster recovery than other teens, and (5) are less likely to use drugs and alcohol.[24] These findings indicate that when children are taught what is right and wrong, and these values are reinforced by the neighborhood and community, they are more likely to make good decisions. Total agreement on what is right and wrong in every community is impossible. However, because bullying is never right, it must be viewed as a community issue, just as developing good character traits has become a focus of many communities.

Poor School Environment

Stephenson and Smith, and Elliot, have discovered a variety of factors in the school environment that may contribute to bullying.[25] Following are some of these factors:

- Low staff morale
- High teacher turnover

- Unclear standards of behavior
- Inconsistent methods of discipline
- Poor organization (in classrooms, on playgrounds, and so on)
- Inadequate supervision (playgrounds, halls, toilets, cafeterias)
- Children not treated as valued individuals
- Not enough equipment (gym class, playgrounds, classroom, labs)
- Lack of support for new students
- Teachers being late
- School personnel leaving classroom during class time
- Intolerance of differences
- Teachers pointing and shouting
- Allowing hurtful graffiti to remain
- Discouraging students from telling on others
- No anti-bullying policy
- No clear procedures for reporting and dealing with bullying incidents
- Bullying ignored by school personnel
- Narrow, dark halls
- Crowded locker rooms
- Lack of support for students with special needs
- School personnel who use sarcasm
- School personnel who humiliate students in front of peers
- No space for quiet activities

The social climate of the school and the quality of supervision provided in the school are of great importance. School climates lacking warmth and acceptance of all students are more likely to have bullying problems and discipline problems. Further, schools lacking high behavioral expectations of students and effective consequences are more likely to create environments where bullies thrive.

Bullying often occurs in areas where there is no adult supervision, not enough adult supervision, or poor quality of adult supervision. Quality supervision in schools is critical. Schools with low levels of supervision experience more bullying. Lack of structure is also often characteristic of the times and places where bullying occurs. For example, time spent in playgrounds, hallways, bus stops, cafeterias, and bathrooms is often unstructured time. Students are relatively free to behave as they wish, within certain parameters.

KEY MESSAGES

- Understanding what causes bullying can help us better address the problem.

- Both bullies and victims are products of our society and are reflections of the quality of our families, schools, and communities.

- There are many possible causes of bullying, ranging from innate preferences to poor home environment to prejudice and desire for revenge.

- The social climate of the school and the quality of supervision and structure provided at your child's school are of great importance.

4

Giving Your Child a Good Start

Dear Dr. Beane:

I never knew parenting would be so difficult. We hear other parents talk about the cruelty of children at school. When I hear them describe how their children are being mistreated and how teachers and principals aren't always supportive, wanting to blame their children, I often think about homeschooling our children or sending our children to Christian schools. If we decide to send our children to the public schools, what can we do to help them have a good start? I hear parents say that once your child is labeled as someone to mistreat, it is difficult to stop the mistreatment. I also want my children to treat others right. What can I do to encourage that?

As good parents, you want your child to have a good start in life. Because you are your child's first teachers, you play an important role in her happiness, physical health, mental health, and ultimate success in life. A quality home life can powerfully influence your child's ability to relate to people and cope with problems in life. For example, providing instruction and experiences that help your child develop self-confidence and give her a healthy self-esteem will help her deal with bullies.

Do unto Others

To begin with, you must do all you can to rear children who value the Golden Rule: treat others the way you want to be treated. The importance of that rule must not be underestimated. It is the foundation of all efforts to prevent and stop bullying. You should teach your child to be kind and not envious or self-centered. Teach your child to rejoice in the success of others and to encourage others. One thing you can do to help your child develop these characteristics is to get her involved in religious activities. When children are involved in such activities, they are less likely to engage in inappropriate behavior.

Communicate your zero tolerance of the mistreatment of others. Let your child know that you value kindness. When you observe good or bad behavior in others, read about it, or see it on television, discuss it with your child. Periodically remind your child that she should tell you when she or someone else is being mistreated at school or in the neighborhood.

Provide Unconditional Love

Give your child plenty of unconditional love and attention. Unconditional love tells your child that you love her for who she is and not for what she does. Tell your child that your love for her will never end. Hug her, smile at her, stroke her hair, pat her on the back, hold her hand, and say pleasant things to her. Indicate that your time with her is precious and valuable. Your love for her will help her love herself and accept herself. Self-acceptance is the basis for self-improvement, and self-love is the basis for compassion toward others. When disciplining your child, focus on the inappropriate behavior instead of criticizing her. Explain that you love her but that you don't like her behavior.

If your child feels that you do not love her, she may think that she doesn't deserve your love. When she feels this way, she may think that she is unworthy of anyone's love. She may even think she should not love herself. Before long, she may think she is a "nobody" who has no value. This is devastating and can have dire consequences.

Be a Good Role Model

Be a good role model by exhibiting self-control, kindness, empathy, and sensitivity. Live the Golden Rule yourself, treating others the way you want to be treated. Of course, there will be times when you are not a good role model. We all have those days. When you find yourself demonstrating inappropriate behavior, immediately apologize to your child and ask for forgiveness. Teach your child the power of apologies and forgiveness. You should teach your child to apologize for bad behavior, regardless of her age, even if child development experts may tell you that your child is too young to know what she is doing. When your child apologizes, give her a hug and tell her you forgive her and love her.

Teach your child to be a peacemaker. Tell her not to be someone who stirs up strife. Ask her not to spread lies and rumors or even true stories that might be hurtful to someone or cause conflict. Striving to be a peacemaker will make your child happier and at peace with herself.

Respect the feelings of your child. For example, don't tease her about her fears, even if they seem silly. Your child's fears seem real to her. If you make fun of her fears, she may not tell you when she is fearful of a serious hurt.

Teach your child the difference between right and wrong, good and bad; surround her with people who have good morals. There are powerful influences in the world today that are trying to snatch your child from you. You must be assertive to counteract the negative influences in our society. Teach your child that it is wrong to hate people, but that it is okay to hate evil and the mistreatment of others.

Provide Time to Rest

Make sure your child gets a good night's rest. The connection between behavior, learning, and sleep is not yet clear, but common sense tells us that adequate sleep is a basic necessity for children's learning and self-control. I have noticed that profoundly sleepy children have impaired impulse control, and some become hyperactive.

Encourage Good Communication

Have one-to-one chats and family meetings around such topics as kindness, love, patience, tolerance, acceptance, sense of belonging, courage, justice, generosity, helpfulness, honesty, honor, respect, respecting and protecting the rights of others, citizenship, empathy, sensitivity, racism, charity, and service. It is also a great time to discuss positive events in the lives of family members and to discuss family responsibilities and rules.

Family meetings are also a great way to promote closeness and unity in your family and to teach problem-solving and decision-making skills. The agenda can be developed jointly with all family members, but one of the parents should chair the meetings. Family meetings help open lines of communication and help family members learn to work together to learn important concepts and solve problems. Family meetings also give children a sense of security, a sense of belonging, and a sense of self-worth; they can be used to enhance a child's self-esteem and self-confidence. These meetings also help children feel that there are parameters in their lives and that they can control certain aspects of their lives. Family meetings also give children a sense of responsibility and accountability.

Try to keep your family meetings to fifteen to thirty minutes in length and meet where there will be few or no distractions. Try to meet once a week. You may want to hold meetings after your youngest children go to bed, until they're ready to participate in the meetings. Reach an agreement with your family on the time and frequency of your meetings and make a commitment not to cancel or miss meetings. You should also establish certain ground rules, such as no interrupting others when they are speaking. Also, try to end all the meetings on a positive note, with a fun activity.

When you see inappropriate behavior in your home, intervene immediately. For example, when one of your children makes a negative comment about another, immediately ask her to make two positive comments. If she will not, make the comments yourself and punish the child for the negative comment. Then tell your children you will not tolerate their using words to hurt someone, and if the mistreatment happens again, you should apply appropriate and serious disciplinary consequences. Be consistent by never letting a put-down occur without your response.

Teach your child to applaud the successes of other family members. When someone does something deserving of recognition, ask the family to join you in applause. Make sure no one in the family is left out; watch for something about each member of the family to bring to everyone's attention. Look for the positive in all your children.

Give your child one-to-one attention. Be a good listener. Good listening is the first step toward being your child's encourager. When you try to be a good listener, it says to your child, "I am very interested in you and what's happening to you, and I want to hear your thoughts and feelings." It is estimated that we spend about 70 percent of our waking hours communicating (reading, writing, speaking, listening), and most of that time goes to listening. However, parents are often poor listeners. When your child speaks, be quiet, lean slightly forward, make good eye contact, don't interrupt, and say things that indicate you understand the feelings being expressed. Empathize and ask questions that demonstrate that you are listening and that you desire to understand what is being said. Stay calm. Do not act upset, even if you are, regardless of what your child shares with you. When you have an emotional reaction, you could make the problem worse. Be sensitive to the fact that your feelings can be expressed through your facial expressions and your tone of voice. In addition, always compliment your child for her willingness to share with you what is going on with her and her life.

Help your child develop good communication skills. Such skills are important in every relationship your child will have. Teach her how to be a good listener, how to communicate her thoughts and feelings appropriately, and how to respond to the thoughts and feelings of others.

Explain the Rules

Have consistent family rules and consequences for breaking rules. The rules should be firm, friendly, fair, enforceable, and age appropriate. Explain your behavioral expectations and the reasons for each rule. Tell your child that the rules are not meant to restrict her, but to make sure she gets the best that life has to offer. The rules are designed to give her freedom from conflict, anger, heartache, and unhappiness. It is important that you be consistent in enforcing the rules. Then be a good model by obeying them yourself. The following are some examples of family rules.

Examples of Family Anti-Bullying Rules

- We treat others the way we want to be treated.
- Bullying is not allowed in our home.
- We don't tease, call names, or put people down.
- We don't hit, shove, kick, or punch.
- We listen to each other's opinions.
- We treat each other with kindness and respect.
- We respect each other's property.

Teach Respect

Teach your child to respect authority, starting with yourself. You are the first authority figure she encounters. If she doesn't respect you, she will not respect others in authority. This requires that you not tolerate disrespect and that you reward and reinforce your child's respectful behavior. Do not allow your child to talk back to you or others in a disrespectful way.

Respect is a two-way street. You cannot expect your child to show you respect if you do not show her respect. Model respect by being a good listener, giving her eye contact when she speaks to you, giving her permission to have a different opinion or preference, giving her approved choices, knocking on her bedroom door before entering, always introducing her to others, and letting her answer questions that are directed to her. When talking to someone else in the presence of your child, do not talk about her as if she weren't there. Also, never belittle, embarrass, or humiliate your child in front of her friends. This is especially important when it comes to discipline. When possible, punishment should be administered away from onlookers.

Provide Supervision

Supervise your child carefully, especially when she is with others. Unsupervised children have more behavior problems. You can't teach and correct your child if you aren't there. This is also a good time to discreetly use the misbehavior of other children as a teachable moment. Children need structure and adult guidance.

Work with other parents to establish a telephone network so that your children can call other parents for help if they cannot reach you. Help your child learn these telephone numbers and other important telephone numbers and names of individuals to call in case of an emergency. Ask her to keep these on a piece of paper in her pocket. Work with other parents in the neighborhood to ensure that children are supervised closely on their way to and from school. Perhaps you can establish "safe homes" or "safe businesses" children can enter to escape a bully or a gang of bullies.

Discipline Your Child with Care

Don't bully your child. Don't physically abuse, overly criticize, demean, or shout at her. Words cut to the heart and are remembered for a long, long time. Use your words to build her up, to encourage and support her, not to cut her down. Avoid making sarcastic and insulting, belittling, or derogatory remarks. No one should be verbally abused. Evaluate and, if necessary, modify your parenting style and disciplining techniques. Your discipline style needs to be designed around the nature and needs of each child. You should never show favoritism or be more lenient with some children, but your discipline strategies may be different for different children. Use positive discipline strategies to help your child feel loved, develop confidence and positive self-esteem, and have a sense of security.

Your approach to discipline should be warm, firm, nonviolent and nonaggressive, and not permissive. You are the key to your child's development of acceptable behavior. James Dobson defines permissiveness as "the absence of authority, resulting in the lack of boundaries for the child."[1] When parents are too permissive, they create children who feel their life is out of control, and the children's behavior often reflects this feeling. When children are not given boundaries, they test inappropriate behavior to see what the consequences are. If the behavior is ignored or allowed, then they still do not know what the limits are. Boundaries are not set only by negative or correcting consequences administered by you. Boundaries can also be set by praising children for good behavior. Therefore, it is important for you to generously praise appropriate behavior observed in your child.

Dobson recommends avoiding the extremes of discipline styles:

> On the side of harshness, a child suffers the humiliation of total domination. The atmosphere is icy and rigid, and he lives in constant fear. He is unable to make his own decisions and his personality is squelched beneath the hobnailed boot of parental authority. Lasting characteristics of dependency, overwhelming hostility, and psychosis can emerge from this overbearing oppression. The opposite position, ultimate permissiveness, is equally tragic. Under this setting, the child is his own master from his earliest babyhood. He thinks the world revolves around his heady empire, and he often has utter contempt and disrespect for those closest to him. Anarchy and chaos reign in his home, and his mother is often the most nervous, frustrated woman on the block.[2]

Some child experts recommend that you provide your child with an appeal process. Sometimes parents have not adequately considered all the facts to determine if the discipline is necessary and appropriate. Parents can make mistakes and may need to apologize and ask forgiveness. Therefore, the child needs an opportunity to present her case in a respectful manner. You and your child should express mutual respect during the appeals process.

Encourage Quality Friendships

Encourage your child to befriend individuals who are kind and accepting of others and to avoid friendships with those who mistreat others. If your child makes friends with individuals you do not approve of, express your concern. If you can't seem to influence her choice of friends, then invite them over. It's better for you to have an eye on them than to wonder where they are and what they're doing. You could even suggest things they could do and places to go. Sometimes children get into trouble because they are bored and are looking for a way to have a good time. You can be a positive influence.

Teach your children to be good friends; encourage them to support their friends and not be jealous of them. Teach your child that there is a difference between a clique and a group of friends. Cliques are often made up of popular children who think they are better than others and are not kind to others. They often establish rules that exclude others and demand loyalty to the clique. Make sure your child understands that many cliques are about power and that being in them is not a goal worth pursuing. Being in a clique means agreeing to reject someone.

Encourage Expression of Feelings

Teach your child to tell you how she feels, to talk about her troublesome thoughts and about what is happening to her, even if she thinks it will make you worry. That is your job. When you decided to be a parent, you agreed to worry about your children for the rest of your life. Especially encourage your child to let you know when someone is hurting her. Tell her you want to know what she is thinking and feeling because you love her with all your mind and heart.

Help your child develop a "feelings vocabulary" when she is young so that she is better able to express her feelings to you. Teach the following list of words to your child and occasionally use these words yourself to express your feelings. When your child is having trouble expressing her feelings, ask her to select the most appropriate word(s).

Feeling Words

Happy	Shocked	Confused
Excited	Terrified	Puzzled
Eager	Restless	Mixed up
Joyful	Calm	Irritated
On top of the world	Content	Mad

Sad	Satisfied	Angry
Down	Proud	Upset
Miserable	Relaxed	Furious
Tearful	Surprised	Fearful
Fidgety	Startled	Embarrassed
Anxious	Shy	Guilty
Tense	Bashful	Self-conscious
Worried	Helpless	Ashamed
Afraid	Lonely	Safe
Hurt	Exasperated	Amazed
Annoyed	Bewildered	

Build Positive Self-Esteem

Respect your child's nature. Your child came "pre-wired," and her "bags were half-packed." This means that she was born with a certain temperament and characteristics. For example, some children have a need to be active and cannot sit still for long periods of time. They are not hyperactive; they are just very active. Some children's personalities are more intense than others—certain feelings and needs are more intense. Some are more sociable than others. Respect and appreciate your child's nature. Don't make her feel that she must transform her nature to be like one of her siblings or you.

Have an "Affirmation Box" in your home. This can be just a shoe box with a slit cut in the top. Leave a pen and small pieces of paper near the box. Once or twice a week, write something positive about your child and place it in the box for her to read. Keep the comments to one or two sentences in length. Encourage all your children to write positive notes about each other. You will probably need to screen the notes before they are read to make sure they really are affirmations. After your child reads the message, explain why you feel she deserves the positive comment. The following list of positive characteristics may help you write your sentences.

Positive Characteristics

Able to resolve conflicts
Alert
Ambitious
Analytical
Appreciative
Articulate
Assertive
Calm
Careful
Caring
Cautious
Cheerful
Confident
Conscientious
Consistent
Cooperative
Courageous
Courteous
Creative
Dedicated
Dependable
Determined
Dynamic
Eager
Efficient
Empathetic
Enthusiastic
Ethical
Fair
Faithful
Focused
Friendly
Fun

Generous
Gentle
Giving
Goal setter
Good example
Good follower
Good leader
Good listener
Good sport
Hard working
Health conscious
Healthy
Helpful
Honest
Honorable
Hopeful
Humble
Humorous
Imaginative
Independent
Industrious
Innovative
Inspiring
Intelligent
Interesting
Intuitive
Inventive
Kind
Knowledgeable
Likable
Lively
Logical
Loving

Loyal
Mature
Mediator
Merry
Motivated
Neat
Nice
Obedient
Open-
   minded
Optimistic
Organized
Patient
Peaceful
People
   oriented
Punctual
Quick
Reasonable
Relaxed
Reliable
Reputable
Resilient
Resourceful
Responsible
Safety
   conscious
Self-assured
Self-
   disciplined
Self-starter
Sensible
Sensitive

Service	Tactful	Unselfish
minded	Tenderhearted	Upbeat
Sharing	Thoughtful	Versatile
Sincere	Tolerant	Willing to
Stable	Trusting	compromise
Strong	Trustworthy	Wise
Successful	Understanding	Witty

If you don't want to use a box, each week simply select a word either from this list or one you come up with that describes your child and mention to her that you have noticed that characteristic in her. Another related strategy is to arrange a situation so that your child overhears you talking positively about her to someone else. Also frequently remind your child of the positive things people have said about her. Use your words and actions to improve your child's self-esteem. Be your child's biggest fan. Let her hear you raving about her positive characteristics. Zig Ziglar says to be a "good-finder."[3] Look for the good in your child and make sure she sees that good.

Teach your child to engage in positive self-talk. You can encourage this by trying to give your child a compliment each day. It is natural for people to say negative things to themselves: "I'm stupid" or "I can't do anything right." Teach your child to become accustomed to saying and hearing positive things about herself.

Avoid criticizing the personality and appearance of your child. Negative adjectives (such as *stupid, clumsy, ugly*) are just as powerful as positive adjectives, and they can have a devastating effect on your child's self-esteem. James Dobson says, "Self-esteem is the most fragile attribute in human nature; it can be damaged by a very minor incident and its reconstruction is often difficult to engineer."[4] Further, when your child hears you use negative words to describe her, she may become resentful. Such feelings toward you may make her feel guilty, causing her to behave inappropriately in the hope of being punished for her feelings.[5]

Avoid asking your child to display her weaknesses in front of others. For example, if she has difficulty reading, don't ask her to read while family members or others are listening. Instead ask her to do something that demonstrates her strengths.

Never give your child negative nicknames or introduce her in a negative way, even if you mean it to be cute or just a joke, such as "This is Shorty," "This is the runt of the family," "This is my little devil," or "This is the stinker of the family." Your words should communicate that you love her and are proud to be her parent. Your child needs to feel that she is important to you.

Your child's self-image and self-esteem are very important. When she feels bad about herself, she does not understand how others can like her or accept her. This thinking hinders her ability to make friends and could lead to depression.

It is also best to avoid labels that are difficult to live up to, such as "This is my little angel" or "This is my little honor-roll student." Just let your child know that you will always love her and that there is nothing she can ever do to change that, good or bad. That's just the way it should be between a parent and child. Making the honor roll doesn't change your love for her. Her failing some of her classes doesn't affect your love for her. Even being an "angel" doesn't change your love for her. Never, never, never make your child feel as if she is a disappointment.

Help your child establish realistic goals and help her understand her purpose in life. Make sure your child doesn't set only long-range goals that take too long to meet. Break them up into short-term goals that lead to each long-term goal. This will provide more opportunities for encouragement, success, and reward. When she meets her goals, celebrate. Reward or reinforce efforts, even if goals are not met. Meeting goals is a great way to enhance self-confidence and pride.

Build Physical Strength

Enroll your child in an exercise program, weight-lifting program, dance class, or martial arts program. These programs build self-esteem and confidence and teach self-respect and respect for others. Before enrolling a child in any program, especially martial arts, ask the instructor if you can observe a few lessons. Also do your homework and ask others in your community about the instructor.

Physical exercise can result in better physical condition and better coordination, as well as help your child deal with stress and anxiety. If you are thinking of choosing martial arts for your child, be aware that although your child may never use the martial skills taught, she will be better prepared to handle and even avoid a physical attack. In other words, martial arts can empower your child. I have been told that kids who learn martial arts seem to develop a sensitivity to potentially hurtful or dangerous situations—as if they have radar. Most martial arts classes emphasize that physically fighting back is a last resort and can in fact make the bullying worse. But if your child is unable to run or be verbally assertive in a situation and finds herself being physically attacked, being trained to respond will help her.

Encourage Positive Thinking

Give your children hope through your vision of them. Successful parents raising positive children need to see (visualize) their kids as someday being competent, positive adults. This positive vision should be shared with your child. This will help your child see herself as a successful adult in the future. This attitude in you and your child will have a positive impact on your behavior and hers. Zig Ziglar says that positive thinking will not let you do anything, but it will let you do everything better than will negative thinking.[6]

Be an encourager. Constantly remind your child of the things she does well. Whenever you see her being good or doing good, let her know you have noticed it. By being an encourager, you draw out the very best in your child. This is especially important when your child doesn't want to be involved in sports and attends a school where sports are emphasized. Make sure your child understands that involvement in sports is not required. Some children feel that others think less of them if they are not involved in sports. Some families and school systems put athletes on pedestals. There is tremendous value to be found in sports, but children should not feel that something is wrong with them because they are not athletes and have no desire to be athletes. Some children get to the point where they dread the question, "What sport are you involved in?" Establish a routine of doing something special for each of your children. For example, on Friday nights play a game with your child or go with her to the movie theater or cook something special for her. Occasionally exceed her expectations by doing something significant—or just give her a significant amount of your time each week.

Build your child's self-confidence by giving her approved choices. Instead of telling her what to do, what to wear, and so on, select two or three options you approve of and ask her to select one. Let your child be a helper at home. Give her responsibilities. She needs opportunities to be responsible for something, whether it be chores or taking care of a pet. This will help her feel competent, valued, and secure. When everything is done for her, she may feel inadequate and insignificant. Be sure to brag about how well she carries out her assigned duties and responsibilities.

Occasionally give your child a nice card or note that expresses your feelings toward her and your desire for her happiness. Leave the card or note where you know she will find it. Tell her that she has been a blessing to you. Most of all, tell her how proud you are of her—not so much for her accomplishments, but for who she is.

Relieve Stress

Tell your child that life can be stressful and teach her ways to prevent and deal with stress. For example, regular exercise and relaxation techniques can help relieve stress. A good diet and positive self-talk can also fend off the negative effects of stress.

Address Behavior Issues

If your child exhibits inappropriate behavior, rule out physical causes, such as attention-deficit disorder, visual or hearing problems, and so on. Make sure a physician annually evaluates your child's physical condition.

Learn to use questions to get at the heart of problem behaviors. Tedd Tripp says that the heart determines behavior and that you must begin by seeking to understand the nature of your child's internal conflict that is expressed in her behavior.[7] Your goal is not only to correct but also to understand the "why" of what has been said and done and the struggle within your child. Try using questions such as the following that work back from the behavior to the heart. As your child answers the questions, your job is to help her understand herself and speak with clarity and honesty about her internal struggles.

Examples of Questions for Discovering the Heart of Behavior Problems

- What were you feeling when you hit your sister?
- What did your sister do to make you mad?
- How does hitting your sister seem to make things better?
- What was the problem with what she was doing to you?
- What is the problem with the way you treated her?
- In what other ways could you have responded?

Teach your child that it is okay to feel anger or any other emotion. However, feelings need to be expressed appropriately. Teach your child alternatives to hurting someone in return for hurting her. Explain some of the following anger management strategies.

Managing Anger

- Accept your angry feelings. See them as normal. Do not try to hide them or ignore them. Tell an adult about them.
- Stop and think. Don't do anything immediately—think about your options.
- Think about how you have the power to control your feelings and thoughts.
- Tell yourself, "It's okay to feel angry, but it's not okay to hurt someone!"
- Look around the room and count and name the objects you see to yourself (such as one class, two pens, four notebooks, and so on).
- Look around the room and find an object and describe it in detail to yourself.
- Put a smooth stone in your pocket; when you get angry, put your hand in your pocket and feel the smoothness of the stone to remind you to calm down.

- Tell the person how you feel.

- Learn to use breathing to help you control anger. Count to ten and take ten deep breaths. Start by standing or sitting straight, then breathe through your nose. When you breathe in, your stomach should go out and you should feel your lungs filling up with air. Make your breaths last a little longer than normal. Hold your breath until you count to three and then let it out slowly while pulling your stomach in.

- Tense and then relax every muscle.

- Just walk away from the angry situation and do something else you enjoy (for example, listen to music you like, run, or take a walk).

- Write a story, song, poem, or letter about your anger.

Teach your child to express her feelings with words in respectful ways and not to act on her angry impulses. It is also important to praise your child for self-restraint and to demonstrate self-control in your own life.

Encourage Hobbies and Talents

Help your child discover a hobby or skill that will make her feel good. Don't let your child sit around moping. It's human nature to focus too much on our problems and weaknesses. Children who don't have something that keeps them busy may tend to have low self-esteem and may become depressed.

Help your child identify her talents and gifts that can be developed. Once a week (or occasionally) ask your child to make a list of the positive things that are happening in her life. This activity may help your child identify her abilities. People tend to enjoy things they are good at or that are rewarding. This effort will also help your child focus on the positives in her life and improve her self-esteem.

Encourage Helping Others and Teamwork

Reinforce and reward accepting behavior observed in your child and make positive comments about her behavior. Let her know that you value kindness, sensitivity, and empathy, especially when they are used to help others. For example, perhaps your child voices her desire to help you make a new family feel welcome in the community. You could work together to meet their needs. If they have children who will be going to your child's school, invite them over to your home to get to know your child. Ask your child to help you make or purchase a greeting card welcoming them.

Involve your child in service or charity projects. There is something emotionally healing about helping others. Occasionally take your child on a family field trip designed to build sensitivity and empathy. Visit a shelter for the homeless, a children's hospital, or a nursing home. Such experiences may even help your child develop teamwork skills or leadership skills.

Teach your child the importance of cooperation, teamwork, collaboration, and appropriate compromise, especially when it is required to help others. Individuals who think they can do everything by themselves or who think they are always right have a difficult time in life. Reward her when you see her cooperating or appropriately compromising with others. Teach her, however, that it is not appropriate to compromise or to go along with an individual or group when they are asking her to do something wrong or questionable.

Avoid Exposure to Violence

Monitor the television viewing of your child. Help your child distinguish between what is real and what is not real on television. According to the Federal Communications Commission, the average American child will witness twelve thousand violent acts on television each year, amounting to about two hundred thousand violent acts by the time he turns eighteen.[8] From 1994 to 1997, a national television viewing study gathered data from almost ten thousand hours of programming and made the following findings:[9]

- 60 percent of sampled programs contained violent scenes.
- More than one-third of violent scenes featured bad characters who were never punished.
- 70 percent showed no remorse or penalty at the time violence occurred.
- 40 percent of all violence included humor.
- 50 percent of the scenes studied showed no pain cues.
- More than 50 percent of the violent incidents would be lethal or incapacitating if they occurred in real life.
- 40 percent of the violence was perpetrated by attractive (hero) characters.
- A typical preschooler watching about two hours of cartoons daily will see ten thousand violent incidents per year, five hundred of which are likely to model aggressive attitudes and behaviors.

More than a thousand other studies confirm a link between heavy television viewing and aggressive behavior, crime, and other forms of societal violence. Studies on television viewing reveal that the amount of violence on television is increasing. Viewing violent programs can make children afraid, worried they may become victims, or suspicious and may increase tendencies toward aggressive behavior. They may also become desensitized to real-world violence. Make a list of the television shows, along with times and channels, that your child has permission to watch each week. As each show is viewed, ask your child to mark through the title.

Lt. Col. Dave Grossman says that we also need to recognize the impact of violence in the news.[10] He says that overexposure to violence in the news can encourage a child to seek violence in entertainment. He goes on to say that the news too often focuses on violence and the negative side of human behavior. Preschoolers should definitely not be allowed to watch the news.

Michelle Elliott, the founder of Kidscape, says you can use television to inspire your child.[11] Certain television shows and movies could inspire your child to play a musical instrument, help the homeless, help starving children, and be kind to those who are mistreated and rejected.

Also monitor your child's use of the Internet and use of violent video games. Refuse to buy or condone violent video games. The earlier video games are introduced, the more likely it is that the child will crave violent ones.[12] Set up your child's computer where you can easily walk by and see what she is working on. Some parents have located their child's computer in a room without a door and have the computer screen facing the hallway.

Also monitor the music your child listens to at home or in the car and refuse to allow your child to play music with violent themes. The Recording Industry Association of America offers the following suggestions for parents:[13]

- Look up the lyrics to songs before allowing your kids to listen to them. There are resources on the Internet.

- Control what children listen to: monitor the music they buy and that they download from the Internet, which is where many kids get their music these days. Turn off the radio if you're turned off by the lyrics. Have an agreement with your children right from the beginning that you have input and power over their decision making on what they listen to and what they buy.

- Listen with your children. See what's there. Respond to it and help them understand and synthesize what they're being exposed to.

- Pay special attention to CDs your child has that have had their labels torn off.

Substitute more appropriate music for music with offensive lyrics. Appropriate music can enhance your child's creativity and problem solving, as well as promote mental relaxation and pleasure.

Protect Your Child from Weapons

The news stories and statistics about accidental shootings are frightening: on an average day in 2002, eight young people were killed by a gun—that's one every three hours.[14] When a child takes a gun to school for protection, victims of bullying stockpile guns and retaliate. Access to guns can be a contributing factor to acts of violence. One middle school teacher told me that she was bullied and tormented for several years in school when she was a child, and she often thought about retaliating. She said, "If I had had access to a gun, I guess I would have killed them." If you have guns in your house,

- Keep guns locked up. If locked with a key, keep the key out of reach.
- Make them difficult to find and impossible for your children to reach.
- Keep them unloaded.
- Store ammunition locked up in a separate place away from the guns.
- Place trigger locks on all guns.

- Teach children that guns kill and that death is permanent.
- Teach your child gun safety, perhaps through a gun safety course.

Explain how your child should act when she sees a friend with a gun: stop, don't touch, get away, and tell an adult. Talk about how to respond to these specific situations:

- A friend shows her a gun.
- A classmate has a gun in his backpack or locker.
- She sees a person walk into the store with a gun.
- She finds a gun.

Be Informed and Involved

Seek information about parenting issues, child development, and today's youth culture. One of the best sources for such information is the Internet. Following is a small sampling of such web sites:

The Center for Parent/Youth Understanding
Walt Mueller, the founder and president, seeks to unite parents and children by helping parents understand youth culture. This site has a strongly Christian perspective. (www.cpyu.org)
Connect with Kids
This site offers great resources for parents and educators. It features articles, videos, and a free newsletter tracking the latest in trends among today's youth culture. (www.connectwidthkids.com)
Great Transitions
This online report represents the culmination of the Carnegie Council on Adolescent Development's ten years of research on the adolescent experience in contemporary culture. The site synthesizes of "the best available knowledge and wisdom about adolescence in America." (www.carnegie.org/sub/pubs/reports/great_transitions/gr_intro.html)
Youth Intelligence
This company is one of many that track youth culture for the purpose of market research. The site is a gateway into the

resources and services that are the fruit of "investigating the lives and interpreting the behavior of Gen X and Gen Y." (www. youthintelligence.com)

RETROspective

This online parents' guide to youth culture comes from the federal department of Health and Human Services. It includes helpful information on changes in youth culture, the power of music, and media literacy. (www.health.org)

Youth Unlimited

This site is filled with valuable youth culture statistics. You will also find archived newsletters with valuable insights into today's youth culture. (www.paulrobertson.ca)

American Academy of Child and Adolescent Psychiatry

This site is loaded with fifty-six up-to-date and concise fact sheets on issues affecting children, teens, and families today. (www.aacap.org)

Encylopedia of Youth Studies

From Dean Borgman and the youth ministry crew at Gordon Conwell Seminary, this is the online home of the Center for Youth Studies and their database of articles on contemporary youth culture. Valuable for parents, pastors, and youth workers. (www.centerforyouth.org)

Search Institute

This site offers practical research, tools, and resources from an organization that's been studying teen values, attitudes, behaviors, and needs since the 1950s. (www.search-institute.org)

Child & Family WebGuide

This is one of the largest clearinghouses of news and research relating to child development and just about any other issue of concern to parents. Operated by Tufts University, the site offers a great selection of links and articles on a variety of teen issues, from bullying and anger management to drug abuse and eating disorders. (www.cfw.tufts.edu)

Passageway

This site is an outreach of the Billy Graham Evangelical Association. From the Q&A page users can send a question to be answered by Passageway staff. The belief and grow links offer archived discussions of essential spiritual and lifestyle resources on topics ranging from church attendance to suicide. (www. passageway.org)

Participate in parenting classes. Find out if community organizations and agencies or your child's school offers classes for parents. If not, start one. Parents often help parents. There are also several web sites whose mission is to help parents develop good parenting skills and to offer guidance on a variety of child-rearing issues.

Stay in touch with your child's school. Attend teacher-parent conferences and other meetings, as well as school events and functions. Ask your child's teacher to keep you informed of all matters relating to your child. Explain to the teacher that you want to be informed about your child's social life and emotional health, not just her academic performance. Keep her teacher informed of events at home that might affect your child's mood, behavior, and learning.

Become a volunteer worker or supervisor at your child's school. Your involvement will help you stay informed, and you can make a tremendous difference. This will communicate to your child that you feel education is important. It will also give you an opportunity to develop relationships with school personnel that could pay off if your child has to deal with troublesome school-related issues.

Talk About Bullying and the Social Environment at School

Discuss the nature of bullying with your child. When you see bullying on television, make sure to discuss it with your child and explain that she should not tolerate it or participate in it. Discuss with your child real-life cases of bigotry and biases presented on television and in other media. Ask her to make notes about bullying, bigotry, and biases she sees on tele-vision and to discuss her findings with you or during a family meeting.

Ask your child to recall a time someone mistreated her, such as when someone's words or behavior hurt her. Also ask her to describe a time when she said or did something to hurt someone, a time when she saw or heard bullying but didn't do anything about it, and a time when she saw or heard bullying and either got help or tried to stop it.

Ask your child if she knows anyone who mistreats others almost every day. Discuss why the bullier might desire to mistreat others. Brainstorm with your child to identify ways she might be able to help this person change. For example, if the bullier likes to have an audience, your child could walk off and refuse to laugh.

Ask your child if she knows anyone who is mistreated almost every day. Discuss how people who are bullied might feel. Brainstorm with your child to identify ways she might be able to help others feel accepted and valued. Teach your child not to let others control her interaction with her peers.

Teach your child to avoid individuals who mistreat her and others. Also make sure she is not tolerating mistreatment just to be accepted by popular students. Explain to your child that popu-larity should never be a goal. It is a by-product of our lives. Explain to your child that decency is more important than social status.

Share stories about your days in school. Share with her the times you tried to fit in and what you learned from your experi-ences. Or tell about the times you stood up for victims of bully-ing or went out of your way to make the mistreated person feel liked.

Teach your child to tell a trusted adult when she is mis-treated or sees others mistreated. Explain that it doesn't have to be her teacher. It can be a secretary, custodian, school resource officer, or another adult in the school. Explain that you would also like to know about such incidents.

Have discussions with your child about school and how she feels about the social environment of the school. Ask, "How are students treating one another?" "How are the teachers treating students?" "Is anyone hurting or embarrassing you?" "Are there any cliques in your school that you wanted to join?" "How are the teachers treating one another?" "How was your bus ride today?" "I notice you don't seem to have been feeling well for a while; is there something you want to tell me?" and other similar questions. Sometimes it is better to ask your child to complete open-ended statements.

Open-Ended Discussion Statements About School

- The thing I like most about school is . . .
- The thing I like least about school is . . .
- The funniest thing I saw at school was . . .
- The funniest thing I heard at school was . . .
- The saddest thing I saw at school this week was . . .

When you hear about another child being bullied, defend that child. Let the parents of the child and the school know about the mistreatment. This will show your child that you are willing to defend others who are mistreated and that you expect her to do the same.

Discuss Peer Pressure

Take a stand against negative peer pressure, and voice your expectations of your child. Teach your child that it is not cool to give in to negative peer pressure. Tell her you expect her not to play that game—doing what "everyone else does," wearing what "everyone else wears," or mistreating individuals whom others mistreat. One of the most powerful ways to withstand negative peer pressure is to learn assertiveness skills. Several assertiveness strategies are presented in Chapter Six in the section "Tips for the Victim of Bullying." Many of these will need to be practiced by your child, perhaps role playing with you or in front of a mirror.

Teach her the value of being her own person and not to worry too much about what her friends think. Once you voice your expectations, you might be surprised that your child (especially if under age thirteen) may stop responding to negative peer pressure.

Avoid Prejudice and Discrimination

Discuss with your child the meaning of the terms *prejudice*, *stereotyping*, and *discrimination*. But first examine your own thoughts and feelings about differences and make sure you are not guilty of communicating these to your children. You need to be a good role model, or your words will be empty.

To stereotype is to assume that every member of a religious, racial, ethnic, or cultural group is the same. When we stereotype people, we don't see them as individuals. Prejudice is using stereotypes to judge others as good or bad, nice or mean, smart or stupid, and so on, before getting to know them. Discrimination is ignoring, avoiding, excluding, or even attacking people just because they are different.

Contrary to popular belief, children are not blind to differences they see in people. At a very early age, children begin to ask questions about the differences they observe. Discuss with your child that it is okay to have opinions, but that it is not okay to like or dislike people just because of their social class, clothing, appearance, color, religion, accent, lifestyle, and so on. Explain that it is how people are on the inside that counts. It is the character of a person that really matters. Children learn how to respond to people's differences from the important adults in their lives, such as you. Be sensitive to the comments of your child, reinforcing positive attitudes and correcting inappropriate comments.

Encourage your child to play with children of different backgrounds and cultures. Involve your child in sports, clubs, summer camps, and community activities where there are children with varied backgrounds and cultures.

Conduct a Yearly Review

Once or twice a year, conduct a review of your child. List things you are pleased with and develop strategies for dealing with areas of concern. The questions listed in Appendix A will give you an idea of the kinds of things you should be asking yourself about your child. This activity will help you develop a child who is resilient, able to deal with difficult people she will meet in life, and able to cope with difficult situations. As you conduct this review, be especially sensitive to your child's social and emotional development. You can find information on stages of child development in books or online.

Enjoy Being with Your Child

Always take time just to enjoy your child, as a gift that has been given to you. As parents we are always concerned about our children, and sometimes we store up questions we need to ask them. Then one day we bombard them. I did that with my son. After he became a young adult, we didn't see him very often, and we were worried about him. One day when I was asking him questions out of love and concern, he turned and looked at me in a loving way and said, "Dad, when I'm with you, just enjoy me, just enjoy me." I took his advice. A few months later, he died. I now value those times I relaxed around him, was his dad, and just enjoyed the beautiful person he was. I didn't know he was going to die and that I would not have that opportunity again on this earth. Someday I will enjoy being in his presence again.

───── **KEY MESSAGES** ─────

- A quality home life can have a significant impact on your child's ability to cope with people and with life.

- Your child needs a lot of unconditional love and attention.

- Teach your child to be a peacemaker.

- Surround your child with people who have good morals.

- Have one-to-one chats and family meetings around such topics as kindness, love, patience, tolerance, acceptance, sense of belonging, courage, justice, and respecting and protecting the rights of others.

- Teach your child to befriend individuals who are kind and accepting of others and to avoid friendships with those who mistreat others.

- Be an encourager and help your child develop self-esteem.

- Help your child relieve stress and find a hobby she enjoys.

- Monitor the television your child watches and the music she listens to.

- Have discussions with your child about bullying and about how she feels about the social environment and climate of the school.

- Enjoy just being with your child.

5

Promoting Your Child's Acceptance

Dear Dr. Beane:

I am contacting you because I am concerned about my son. He is only six years old and is already a target of mistreatment, just about any time he gets around other children. Some friends have hinted that he doesn't know how to interact with other children. They say things like, "Don't worry about it, someday he'll learn how to play with others." I've tried to take an honest look at him as he plays with other children. I now realize that there are some things he needs to do differently. He seems to irritate other kids and he always wants his way. I feel like I need to help him learn how to make friends. I'm not sure I know how to do that. What do you recommend? What else can I do to help him be treated right by his friends?

The need to be accepted demands to be met. Children will perpetually seek ways to meet that need—and many of those ways are inappropriate and destructive. Children often look in the wrong places and to the wrong people. You must do all you can to help your child find appropriate ways to gain the acceptance he needs without compromising his beliefs.

Many of the suggestions presented in the previous chapter will not only help you provide a quality home life for your child but also promote the acceptance of your child by helping him become a person whom others want to be around. The following additional strategies may also help your child develop solid, lasting friendships.

Children who have at least one good friend are less likely to be bullied or are bullied for a shorter period of time.[1] This is especially true when a good friend sticks up for them. If your child has at least one good friend, he will also be better able to cope with any bullying he experiences. Your child's friend is likely to be around to witness the bullying and will be able to provide support for your child.

Teach your child good manners and social skills. These will help promote his being accepted. When a child has poor manners and social skills, bullies notice and seek to test him, to see if he is an easy target for mistreatment. These skills will also help your child develop friends who can support him. Review the following list of characteristics of potential victims of bullying. Some, such as race and disability, cannot be changed. But others can be improved or at least mitigated.

- Is somehow different (for example, has a disability, has big ears or an unusually shaped nose, is overweight, is of a different race or religious background, is smaller and weaker than peers, is gifted)

- Is clumsy, uncoordinated, and poor at sports

- Has poor manners and social skills

- Has poor hygiene; wears dirty or ill-fitting clothes

- Teases, pesters, and irritates others, eggs them on, doesn't know when to stop

- Is passive, timid, quiet, shy, and overly sensitive

- Is cautious, clingy, and insecure

- Has few or no assertiveness skills

- Has low or no self-confidence and self-esteem
- Is irritable, disruptive, aggressive, quick tempered
- Lacks sense of humor or uses inappropriate humor

Teach your child how to make friends by sharing the following tips:

Tips for Making and Keeping Friends

- Say hello and smile.
- Be a good listener.
- Be kind to others.
- Tell others about your interests.
- Be honest.
- Be a volunteer and get involved in activities in your community.
- Join clubs and organizations at your school and in your community.
- Ask questions that let people know that you're interested in them.
- Be cooperative and do not insist on always having your way.
- Be willing to share your property and respect the property of others.

Also discuss the following "friendship busters" with your child:

Friendship Busters

- Bragging
- Name-calling
- Being bossy
- Teasing

- Making fun of others
- Being stuck-up
- Spreading rumors and lies
- Stealing
- Being rude
- Ignoring people
- Making people feel left out
- Cheating
- Hitting
- Pinching
- Shoving
- Embarrassing people
- Trying to get people to do things they don't want to do or shouldn't do

Teach your child that sometimes friendships just do not work out. Sometimes you find a friend for a lifetime, and sometimes you have a friend for only a few days. If your child tries his best to be friends with someone and his efforts are not successful, explain that he shouldn't take it personally. Perhaps it just wasn't meant to be. Teach your child how to select good friends, and share the following "Friendship Boosters," a list of the characteristics of a good friend.

A Good Friend

- Is always there for you
- Is someone who listens
- Is someone who likes you for who you are
- Is someone you can trust
- Is fair and honest

- Encourages you to do your best
- Understands you
- Shares with you
- Respects your property
- Sticks up for you
- Doesn't try to get you to do things you shouldn't do

Dispose of any of your child's T-shirts and other clothing that may cause friction at school or in the community. These are clothes with derogatory words and symbols on them. It is not unusual for children to purchase such clothing and hide it. Sometimes they leave for school wearing these items under other clothes; once on the bus, they take off a layer of clothing to reveal the derogatory messages.

Make sure your child's clothes are not out-of-date or too small. If you cannot afford new clothes, many school systems and communities have organizations willing to provide your child with appropriate clothing. You should not feel shame about asking for assistance.

Teach your child to sample friends and play partners and not to be too eager to play only with the popular children. Teach your child how to enter a group by being cooperative and not bossy. Tell your child not to barge in, but to gradually enter a group and just listen until the time seems right to say something. Tell him not to insist that the group do what he wants.

Openly point out your child's positive similarities with other children. The key word here is "positive." It is a good feeling to know you have something in common with others that is viewed as a positive trait. Sometimes this similarity helps a child make friends.

If your child has a disability, inform him about the cause and nature of the disability so that he can talk intelligently and openly about it. When your child seems to accept his disabilities, others feel more comfortable and are more accepting.

Help your child have positive expectations regarding his acceptance and ability to make friends. Ask your child to practice visualizing (seeing) himself getting along with others. Children with such expectations are more likely to engage in behavior that promotes their acceptance. Their interactions with others are more positive.

Reward your child for treating others the way he wants to be treated. This reinforces positive behavior in your child. Positive reinforcement of desirable behavior is sometimes more powerful than punishing a behavior. Of course, both are important. Strike a balance.

Use photographs effectively. When you see your child interacting appropriately with someone, take a picture and give a copy to him and the other child. Social psychologists tell us that this strategy can help a person feel accepted by the individuals in the photograph.

As mentioned in Chapter Four, helping your child develop his interests, learn a new hobby, or develop a skill, such as painting, drawing, or playing an instrument, will help him feel good about himself. It can also help him develop additional friends, either others who share his interests or those who respect that ability. Kids who have interests and skills are more likely to be accepted by others.

If you have a special hobby or skill, give a presentation at your child's school. Or volunteer for responsibilities that the children value, such as serving as the class entertainment coordinator. It might net some social prestige for your child. What children think about parents sometimes rubs off on the parents' children. Of course, this means that you could also bring unwanted attention to your child, so be sensitive to what reaction you are likely to get from your child's peers.

Learn as much as you can about your child. That sounds like a strange thing to ask parents to do, but you may be surprised by what you don't know about your child. The more you know about your child, the more you can show that you are interested in and care about what he cares about. It will also make you better able to talk to your child about what's going on in his life. Ask your child to finish the statements you have selected from the list here. Not every statement may be appropriate for your child, and you may want to add your own questions to the list.

My Favorite

- My favorite TV show is . . .
- My favorite place to go is . . .
- My favorite thing to do in my free time is . . .
- The thing I like MOST about school is . . .
- The thing I like LEAST about school is . . .
- My favorite athlete is . . .
- My favorite radio station is . . .
- My favorite food is . . .
- My favorite place to eat is . . .
- I like people who . . .
- I don't like it when people . . .
- My favorite magazine is . . .
- My favorite book is . . .
- My favorite movie is . . .
- My favorite web site is . . .
- My favorite color is . . .
- My favorite song is . . .
- The job I'd like to have when I grow up is . . .
- My favorite game is . . .
- My greatest hope is . . .
- My biggest worry is . . .

- I am happiest when . . .
- If I could go anywhere in the world, I'd go to . . .
- My favorite type of music is . . .
- My favorite singer, group, or musician is . . .
- My favorite actor or actress is . . .
- The person I admire most is . . .

KEY MESSAGES

- Children who have at least one good friend are less likely to be bullied or are bullied for a shorter period of time.

- Teach your child good manners and social skills.

- Teach your child how to make friends.

- Teach your child to sample different friends and play partners and not to be too eager to play only with the popular children.

- Help your child have positive expectations regarding his acceptance and ability to make friends.

- Reward your child for treating others the way he wants to be treated.

- Get to know your child's likes and dislikes.

6

Helping Your Bullied Child

Dear Dr. Beane:

Our son is being bullied and I wanted to contact you to get your opinion. I told my son and my wife that he should stand up for himself and fight the bully. My wife says that is the wrong kind of advice to give him. We disagree on this issue. What is your opinion? Do you know of any research that proves that fighting back improves one's self-esteem? We are concerned about him and afraid that he might harm himself. So, I think my recommendation is best because it will make him feel good about himself.

The gentleman's opinion in this e-mail message is not uncommon. As I mentioned in the Preface of this book, when my son, Curtis, was in seventh grade, he was bullied and I recommended that he fight the bully. I know what it is like to have a child who is persistently mistreated and not to know what to tell him. I didn't know what to do myself. For some strange reason, I dealt with the problem as if it were only his problem. At first I told him to ignore the bully. He tried to ignore him for several weeks, but it didn't work. One day, the school counselor called me and said Curtis was an emotional wreck and that I needed to take him home. As we sat in our house, I saw the tears and the deep hurt in his face. I didn't know what to tell him to do. I just knew that the bullying had to stop.

I told him to fight back physically—to retaliate. I also told Curtis that he had to win this fight. The next day, the bully started smacking my son around. My son fought back and won the fight. However, in retaliation the bully turned several boys against my son. Later my wife and I discovered that our son sat in the cafeteria by himself for weeks. We transferred him to a larger middle school in a different school system—in the middle of seventh grade. He found acceptance and a sense of belonging in the new school.

At fifteen years of age, he was in an auto accident. He lost two fingers and one-third of his right hand. His other fingers had to be repaired and rebuilt. Several months later, he returned to high school. There was a tremendous outpouring of love and support from some students. However, an unbelievable number of students were cruel to him. This mistreatment took its toll, even into the adult years. At the age of twenty-three, Curtis was diagnosed as suffering from posttraumatic stress from the car wreck and from the persistent mistreatment. He suffered depression and anxiety problems. He came to our home and told us that he had not been out of his bedroom for three days and wanted us to pray for him. We prayed and took him to the doctor. A few weeks later, he called me and said, "Dad, I found some new friends, but they do things I don't agree with." Curtis looked for friendship with the wrong people. One night he took an illegal drug, and it killed him. He had a heart problem that he and we didn't know about. He didn't kill himself. He had his car keys in his hands and was trying to go for help.

My son's life experiences drove me to search for ways to help other children who are bullied and their parents. After much research into bullying, I developed the Bully Free Program, which has been adopted by schools around the United States. I speak to thousands of students and parents about bullying every month and train school personnel in how to implement our program.

I was wrong to tell my son to ignore the bully, and I was wrong to tell my son to retaliate. I know that now. I hope you handle your child's bullying situation better than I did. I wish I had known about the information provided in this book before my son was bullied.

I now know how to prevent and stop bullying. I can't help my son, but I can help you help your child.

Where to Begin

First, be assured that you can help your child. When you find out that your child is a victim of bullying, there is a lot to consider. There are things you can do at home and things you can do in collaboration with your child's teachers and the school. There may even be times when you have to call in the police. But the best thing to do right away is talk to your child about what's going on.

Be thankful that you know about the bullying. Children usually don't tell their parents. If your child told you about the problem, praise her for letting you know and for asking for help. This will encourage your child to keep the communication lines open. Lack of communication is one of the biggest obstacles to preventing and stopping bullying. The more time you spend discussing the mistreatment with your child, the easier it will become for your child to talk about it. Be careful about labeling your child a victim. Having a background in special education, I have learned to dislike labels. We should just identify the strengths and problems that a child has and address them. If we label children as victims, they may seek to behave like victims.

Be prepared for your child, especially if she is a teenager, to ask you not to get involved. Your child may be embarrassed by your involvement or fearful that you will make the bullying worse. This makes it a tough call for you. Your lack of involvement may mean that the bullying will continue for a while. Trust your judgment and the judgment of your child. If you decide not to get involved, be very observant and watch for signs that the bullying is beginning to take a toll on your child.

There may come a time you need to intervene. When this time comes, reassure your child that you will do your best to help without making it worse or embarrassing her. Explain that you love her too much to stand by and watch her be hurt, perhaps even scarred for life by the meanness of others.

Stay calm even though you are concerned. Try not to communicate that you are upset or angry, even though you are. When you have an emotional reaction, you can make the problem worse by making your child fear that you may not handle the situation appropriately. This means you will need to guard your facial expressions and other nonverbal signals, as well as voice tone. It's natural to want to blame someone, but it's best not to be too quick to blame anyone. If your first response is to blame someone, you may not listen as well as you should. Don't respond until your child shares the details of the whole story.

If your child says "No one likes me at school," don't simply disagree, even if you think it will make her feel better. If you disagree with your child too quickly, she may feel that you are not going to be able to help her. She may also decide to hide her feelings. Be sensitive to the fact that your child may feel embarrassed and ashamed. It is difficult for her to admit that no one likes her and that she cannot handle the situation on her own. Also be sensitive to her anxieties, fears, and dread. These are real and make it difficult for her to go to school and to feel safe. These feelings may be so intense that they interfere with her learning, social development, and physical and emotional health.

Don't be embarrassed yourself. I hope this recommendation sounds strange to you. Unfortunately, some parents are embarrassed that their child has trouble being accepted or doesn't stand up for herself.

No matter how minor the event seems to be, take it seriously. What you consider minor may seem devastating to your child. Listening carefully may also help you uncover more severe bullying events in your child's life.

Find Out What Has Happened

Be careful when asking your child to describe the bullying. Avoid making "you" statements; your child may feel she is being attacked. Also keep in mind that not every moment is a great time to talk. When the time seems right, ask your child about the mistreatment she is receiving. Be sure to listen to your child's description of what happened, without interrupting. Without overwhelming your child with questions, try to get the answers to some of the following.

Questions to Ask Your Child

- Who was involved?
- What was said and done to your child by whom?
- What happened or usually happens immediately before the bullying occurs?
- Who were the bystanders, and what did they say and do?
- When did the bullying occur?
- Where did it happen?
- Was there any adult supervision?
- Are there video cameras in the area recording activities?
- How did your child respond?
- What happened or usually happens after the bullying event?
- Who has been told about the bullying, and what have they done (if anything)?
- How long has this been occurring?

Avoid having a knee-jerk reaction to your child's comments. After listening, ask questions to fill in the information gaps, but don't interrogate your child. Don't overload her emotionally by asking too many questions at once. During the process of listening to her, you may discover why she is being mistreated. If not, wait until you think the time is right to ask why she thinks the bullying happens. If you ask too soon, your child may not share everything with you or may not tell the truth. Yes, even good kids lie to their parents. It is important to have the facts about what has happened. Sometimes children leave out critical information that affects our understanding of what occurred. Keep in mind that the "Why did you . . . ?" line of questions rarely works with anyone, even adults. Your child may not even know why she is being mistreated, so don't push her to give you a reason.

Find out what other parents and students know about the bully or bullies. When you talk to them, don't mention the bullying; just seek information in an informal way. Don't criticize the bully or bullies.

Express confidence to your child that you, the adults at her school, and she will be able to find a solution. Explain that there are several things that can be tried, some immediately and some that will take time to implement.

Log and Journal

Keep a log (record) of the bullying events, addressing as many of the questions previously listed as you can. This will make it easier for you to check the facts as you gather more information and hear information repeated. The log will also eliminate the necessity of remembering all the details of every episode.

Ask your child to write down in a journal or notebook her thoughts and feelings about what has happened. Ask her permission to read what she has written. Journaling helps your child work through her emotions and thoughts about her mistreatment. You can then cross-check her journal notes with your conversations with her and with the information shared by others.

Discuss Why Bullying Happens

We've discussed this topic in other chapters, but it deserves repeating here. Make sure your child understands that no one deserves to be bullied and that bullies mistreat a lot of people, not just her. Even though she may already know this, it is good to hear it from you. Explain that children bully others for a lot of reasons, including the following:

- They may be angry because of personal problems.
- They may have been mistreated themselves.
- They may have weak self-control.
- They may have learned that hurting others is a good way to feel powerful and in control.
- They may have parents who have modeled aggression and inappropriate ways of expressing feelings.
- They want to be number one—popular.

Explain that some bullies seek certain reactions. For example, crying and becoming upset may only encourage the bully. It is best that the bully not know she has hurt your child or made her upset.

Let your child know that it is normal to feel hurt, fear, and anger. It is especially important not to make light of her fear. Discuss the importance of expressing feelings and not holding them in. When feelings are kept inside of us, they can upset us more and possibly make us ill. However, it is important for her to express her feelings in an appropriate manner. Explain that you will show her appropriate ways to express these feelings, such as through writing stories, poetry, and songs, as well as through dance, art, and music. Physical activity also can sometimes help a person work through her feelings.

Cheryl Dellasega and Charissee Nixon, the authors of *Girl Wars*, recommend helping your child develop coping skills that do not involve others, such as listening to music, exercising, and keeping a journal.[1] These are activities that will teach your child to channel some of her frustrations and negative energies expressively.

Monitor your child's conversations on the computer and on the telephone. It's fine for the child to share her experience with others, but students who rehash bullying events over and over with others on the telephone and on the computer are more likely to retaliate.[2]

Deal with a Bully's Parents

Avoid being a "fix-it" dad or mom by immediately calling the bully's parents. Use your own judgment about calling them. If you know them well, you may choose to talk to them. Most of the reports I have received from parents indicate that it is usually best not to call the bully's parents unless you are *certain* they will believe you and try to address the problem in a way that will not make the situation worse for your child. However, do not assume that the bully's parents are bad parents. Many parents of bullies are already aware of their child's behavior and are extremely concerned about it.

If you do decide to call the bully's parents, do not call while you are upset or angry. Try to use a soft and calm voice. Don't be judgmental. During the conversation, when you feel the time is best, express your desire to work with the parents to figure out a way your children can get along. At some point, tell the bully's parents that if it were your child who was mistreating someone, you would like to know. Also tell the parents that if they find out that your child is contributing to the problem, you want to know. Don't blame the parents of the bully—they didn't bully your child.

If you talk to them, make sure your goal is to enlist their assistance and not to condemn their child or to get their child punished. Focus on the child's behavior and not on her personality or character. Also, do not exaggerate what is happening to your child. Expect some questions about what is happening and the accuracy of what you have heard. It may be that they have already heard different versions of what is happening. Refer to your notes and try to avoid arguing if there are discrepancies.

Arguing with the parents will only make the bullying worse, and your child will suffer the consequences.

Initially you might say something nonthreatening, such as "Hi, Susan. I've heard about some conflict between Bob and John. I don't believe we should overprotect our children, and I think that they need to learn how to resolve some of their problems, but this sounded serious enough that I thought it was time for us to talk about it so we can help our children. I've been told that Bob is teasing John about his big ears, and this seems to happen almost every day. I know you would not approve of that, so that's why I'm here."

Depending on the age of the children and how well they know each other, consider discussing with the parent the appropriateness of having the children meet to resolve the conflict. Such a meeting is not always effective. If the parents do not agree to arrange a meeting and the bullying occurs at school, then report it to the school. If you decide to arrange a meeting, practice with your child what to say at the meeting. Both of the children's parents should attend the meeting. Toward the end of the meeting, make sure there is some commitment from the bully that the behavior will stop. If your child is provoking the bully, make sure your child makes a verbal commitment to stop provoking her.

You may find the parents receptive, or they may not be willing to accept the fact that their child is mistreating others. It is natural for parents to defend their children. When parents hear their child's behavior being questioned, they sometimes perceive it as an attack on their parenting and as an accusation that they have somehow failed. Parents come up with all kinds of excuses to rationalize their children's behavior. For example, it isn't unusual to hear them say, "Well, I'm sure he really didn't mean anything by that," "Well, he's young and doesn't understand what he's doing. He'll learn as he gets older," "Oh, I see other children do that all the time. I'm sure it's nothing to worry about," and "No, I don't believe my child would do that."

How Your Child Should Respond

Don't tell your child to retaliate. Even children know that their parent's recommendation to "fight back" is not the answer, as this ten-year-old observed:

> When I was being bullied, my dad told me that when he was a kid, if anyone ever hit him, he just hit them back so hard and so many times, they left him alone. He said I had to stand up for myself and the best way to do that was with my fists. I don't think I should hurt someone just because they have hurt me. After my dad told me that, I never let him know again that I was being bullied. There was no way that I could beat up the bully. When my dad asked me how things were going, I would just say okay.

There are several reasons you should not tell your child to retaliate. Telling your child to retaliate teaches her that violence is the way to deal with violence. In most cases, retaliation makes bullying worse and last longer. You also run the risk of your child or the bully being seriously hurt. Your child may try to find a way to equalize the imbalance of power that exists because the bully is stronger and meaner than she. To accomplish this, your child may use a weapon or surprise the bully with a dangerous push in order to harm or even kill the bully. When you tell your child to retaliate, you are also telling her that she is alone in this struggle. That is not the way it should be; adults should get involved.

Don't tell your child to ignore the bully. That usually doesn't work because when victims try to ignore the bully, they are silent and often appear hurt, which prolongs the bullying. The bully usually just works harder to hurt your child by saying meaner and nastier things and by becoming more physical in her attacks. Also, if this approach doesn't work, your child may not come back to you for more ideas. If you do tell your child to ignore the bully, ask her to try ignoring for a week or two and to report back to you regarding its effectiveness.

Show your child the following tips for handling and responding to the bullying. Role-play bullying situations to give your child practice in using the strategies. Another approach is to have your child practice the assertiveness strategies in front of a mirror. It may be necessary for your child to practice several times for two or more days, especially if she lacks self-confidence. Rehearsing the strategies will give her the confidence she needs to use them with the bully. Keep in mind that no one strategy works in all situations for all children. Because you know your child best, you are the best person to help your child select the strategies that will work best for her.

Tips for the Victim of Bullying

- Talk openly and honestly with your parents or a trusted adult about the mistreatment. If the bullying is occurring at school, tell an adult there. If you wish, take a friend with you, but go when the bully is not around. If you cannot tell someone personally about the bullying and how it makes you feel, then write a note to that person explaining what has happened. You can also ask that the person keep your name confidential.

- Don't get defensive if your parents or other adults increase their supervision of your activities. Be thankful that you have adults who care about you.

- Don't retaliate. Don't fight back. Retaliation usually makes bullying worse and last longer. You also run the risk of getting seriously hurt or hurting the bully and getting into trouble with the law.

- Don't be afraid to share with your parents what you think needs to be done.

• Realize that you are not expected to deal with bullying alone. It's not just your problem; parents and other adults should get involved. It has been proven over and over that when adults get involved, bullying can be reduced and stopped.

• When possible, stay calm and cool and don't let the bully know that she has upset you. The bully wants to upset you. Imagine yourself surrounded by a magical, anti-bully shield. This may help you stay calm. Keep an object in your pocket— such as a smooth rock—that you can rub when you are fearful, upset, or angry. This will help you think before you say or do something that causes you more problems.

• Keep in mind that no one deserves to be bullied. Bullies have a need for power and control over others and a desire to hurt people. Sometimes bullies also feel bad about themselves, but not always. Sometimes bullies are bullied at home by their parents or siblings and are determined not to be bullied at school, so they choose to bully others.

• Avoid the bully as much as possible, especially in places where the bully is known to hang out or where there is not much adult supervision. If you cannot avoid the bully, at least try to keep your distance. Give the bully space.

• Try not to be alone anywhere. Hang out with friends or adults. When you see the bully walking toward you, walk over to some individual and start a conversation with her or walk into a crowd.

• If you are being bullied while walking to and from school or while riding the bus, tell your parents and ask them to take you to school or make arrangements for you to carpool to school. Your parents can also ask the school to provide an adult to ride the bus or to let you ride a different bus. Sit near the bus driver and ask a friend to sit with you. If you walk to school, take a different route, but make sure this route is safe.

• If you are bullied in the lunchroom, avoid sitting near those who bully you, or ask a friend to move with you to a different seat. If this is not allowed, ask the lunchroom supervisor if you can move. If the supervisor says you cannot move, ask your parents to speak to someone at school and explain why you must not sit near the bully.

- Be careful to whom you give your phone number(s) and e-mail address(es). If you are being bullied through electronic devices, such as the cell phone or over the Internet, tell your parents. They can report the cyberbullies to the police. Harassing and threatening messages are against the law. If possible, print the messages. Don't respond to a bully's messages. If you are in a chat room and someone starts mistreating you with words, don't respond. Write down her screen name and tell your parents.

- Practice not looking like an "easy target." Bullies often look for potential victims who look like easy targets because they are smaller, physically weaker, nicer, or more sensitive than the bully. Check your body language. Bullies look for people who look sad, who are stooped over, who avoid eye contact with people, who are always fidgeting, who always want to be alone, who might cry easily, and who will not stand up for themselves. Practice looking, walking, and talking like a confident person. Look like a person who is physically and emotional strong. Stand up straight, hold your head up straight, hold your shoulders back, look into the eyes of the bully (not at the ground or somewhere else), use a firm and strong voice, and stay calm. If you make an assertive comment to the bully, walk away with confidence. Don't hang around. If you are not there, you cannot be bullied.

- Don't let those who bully you make you feel bad. Don't say things to yourself like, "I'm ugly," "I'm dumb," or "I can't do anything right." When the bully says something bad about you, say something positive to yourself—reminding yourself of your positive characteristics. If this is difficult for you, ask an adult who loves you to help you make a list of your positive characteristics. Sometimes others see qualities in us that we don't see.

If you wish, tell them why you need help. Always keep a list with you of the positive things in your life and of your positive characteristics. Ask an adult to help you develop these lists.

• If you have to interact with the bully, be assertive by moving closer to the bully, but no closer than an arm's length. Keep a safe distance. You should also turn sideways, relax your hands and arms, and hold them down at your side. You don't want the bully to think you want to fight. Keep your feet about shoulder width apart—for good balance. When you stand this way, you are ready to walk away from the bully or even run if you have to protect yourself.

• In responding to the bully, don't argue or get into a shouting match. Make a firm and assertive statement, telling the bully how you feel, why you feel the way you do, and what you want him to do. Practice and learn to do this with a confident and determined voice. For example, "I feel angry when you call me names because I have a real name. I want you to call me by my real name. My name is Allan." Say this with confidence while you look the bully in the eye, then walk away with confidence. If you are not there, you cannot be bullied.

• Let the bully know you are not an easy target. Stay calm and say to the bully with confidence and determination, "Stop it! Leave me alone." Or you might say, "No! You cannot have my pencil. I need it." Then walk off with confidence. If you are not there, you cannot be bullied.

• The bully wants to hurt your feelings. So act like it doesn't hurt. Don't reward the bully with your tears. Practice having a blank expression on your face. You can also disappoint the bully by admitting she is right. For example, when the bully calls you "fatty," look the bully in the eye and say calmly, "You know, I *am* overweight. I need to start working out with weights." Then calmly walk off with confidence. If you are not there, you cannot be bullied.

• Make an asset of the bully's comment. For example, a bully made fun of a boy who had cancer and lost all his hair because of the treatments. The bully called him "bowling ball." So the boy said, "I guess Michael Jordan and I have something in common."

• Disarm the bully with humor. This doesn't mean you should laugh at the bully. Don't target the bully with your sense of humor. If you do, the bully might think you are making fun of her. Just smile and walk away or say something about yourself as it relates to what the bully said. For example, if the bully makes fun of your ears, you could say, "You know, you're right, my ears stand out like opened doors on a car." The bully might think what you said was funny and leave you alone. Also, individuals with a sense of humor have an easier time than those who let teasing get to them. Having a sense of humor may make the bullying disappear. However, use your best judgment.

• Exhaust the topic by asking the bully several questions. For example, one girl was made fun of because she was overweight. The bully said she was "fat." So she asked, "What do you mean by fat?" "How fat do you have to be to be fat?" "How many people do you know who are fat?" The bully got tired of her questions and left her alone.

• In response to the bully's comments, just keep saying "So what?" It is amazing how powerful that phrase can be. Don't say it so much that it just makes the bully angrier, however. Use your own judgment about when it is time to stop and walk away with confidence.

• Respond to a bully's teasing and name-calling with a non-defensive question: "Why would you say that?" or "Why would you want to say . . .?"

• Yelling can sometimes be effective when you yell exactly what it is you specifically want the bully to stop doing. However, it should be a forceful, assertive yell and not one that expresses hurt or helplessness. For example, you might yell out "Stop hitting me!" instead of "Leave me alone." This will draw attention to the situation and exactly what is happening.

• Be kind to the bully. Your kindness may surprise or confuse her. If you are lucky, it will make her feel shame for mistreating you and encourage her to change the way she treats others.

• Compliment the bully. For example, if the bully says you are too short, say "I know—I wish I were tall like you." This may surprise and disarm the bully.

• Try to distract the bully by starting a conversation about something the bully enjoys talking about. For example, you might ask, "Hey, did you see the Lakers game last night? Did you see that play with two seconds left on the clock?"

• Write down all the things that bullies have said to you. Under each statement, write down assertive comebacks or actions (or both) that might stop the bully from making the comments. This will prepare you for the next time you are bullied.

• Write down all the comments the bully has said to you and then rip the paper into small pieces, as if they were meaningless and no longer a part of your past.

• Remember: you are powerful. You are powerful because you have the power to make a choice. You can let the bullying bother you, or you can choose not to let it get to you. You don't have to give up your power of choice. Just because you choose not to let it bother you doesn't mean you choose to let it continue. You should tell an adult what's going on.

• Use your best judgment and follow your instincts. For example, if the bully wants your homework and you think she is about to punch you, give up your homework, then walk off with confidence and act as if the bully didn't hurt you. Your safety is more important than your possessions. Be sure to tell a trusted adult what happened.

• Tell your friends who are bigger and stronger than the bully about the bullying. When you find the bully alone, take your friends with you and tell the bully to leave you alone. Don't start a fight, but be assertive.

• Try not to take a lot of money or expensive items to school or to places in the community where you will see the bully. If the bully threatens you to get your money or your property, give it up and tell your parents or another trusted adult. You can also ask that they keep your name confidential.

• Label the things you take to school with a permanent marker. The bully is less likely to want to steal them.

• Being bullied can make you tired and make you feel sick. To deal with the bully, you need to feel good, so be sure to get plenty of exercise and eat healthy foods. Also make sure you get plenty of sleep.

• Don't expect to be mistreated. When you are walking toward a group of students, think about them being nice to you and try to see in your own mind them being nice to you. Also do your best to be friendly to them. Treat others the way you want to be treated. Practice visualizing (seeing) yourself getting along with others.

• Stand up for other students who are being bullied and ask them to stand up for you.

• Try to make friends with others at school and outside school. However, be careful whom you select to be your friends. They should be kind people who seek to do what is right, who support you and encourage you to do what is right.

• Develop an interest, hobby, or skill that will make you feel good about yourself and that other kids will think is neat. Then do what you love doing.

• Ask your parents and teachers to help you cope with your feelings and thoughts, focusing on your hurt, fear, loneliness, depression, anxiety, anger, hate, rage, and perhaps desire for retaliation or revenge. Don't try to deal with these alone. Even adults need help dealing with such feelings and thoughts.

• Take a good honest look at yourself. Is there something you need to change about the way you act around others? Are you too aggressive? Are you too bossy? Are you rude and always interrupting others? Ask your parents and teachers to help you develop behaviors that will help you be more accepted. Of course, regardless of your behavior, you don't deserve to be mistreated. Bullying is not your fault. But you may be able to improve on your situation by changing a few behaviors.

• Let your parents help you find good e-mail friends and pen pals.

• Make friends with extended family members: aunts, uncles, cousins, and so on. Do fun things with them. Share your feelings and thoughts with them.

• Ask your parents to buy you a pet. Your pet will always be glad to see you and love you. Your pet can be a great friend.

• Some students join in on the bullying, but they are not really true bullies. They may not realize that they are hurting you. Talk to these individuals and explain how the bullying makes you feel. Explain to them that you understand why they join in—they are afraid they might be the next victim. Tell them that you believe they are good people with good hearts and that you would like for them to be your friend. You may be surprised. They may apologize to you and even come to your defense in the future. Of course, you must be selective in choosing these individuals and say these things only to those for whom you believe it to be the truth. Don't try to befriend those who don't deserve to be your friend. Just treat them the way you want to be treated.

• If you have tried several anti-bullying strategies and nothing seems to help, talk with your parents about the possibility of transferring to a different school or school system. Sometimes this helps, but sometimes it doesn't.

• Tell a trusted adult when you see someone being mistreated. If you wish, take a friend with you, but go when the bully is not around. If you are worried about putting yourself at risk, write an anonymous note to an adult. If you cannot tell your parents, then tell your grandparents, uncle, or aunt—any adult you trust. Tell this adult what is happening, who is involved, who the bystanders are, where it is happening, and when it is happening.

• Maintain open lines of communication with your parents and adults at school. Keep them up-to-date on your mistreatment.

• Don't give up; keep asking for help. If the bullying contin- ues, keep a trusted adult (especially your parents) informed and ask for their assistance. Don't feel that you are causing trouble.

• Maintain hope. Life is always changing, and no one can see the future. No matter how bad life may seem right now, peace and happiness can fill your life in the near future. There are people around you who care about you and want to help you. Trust them.

Help your child work out a plan for responding to the bully- ing in the various situations and locations where it occurs. Teach your child to be assertive, but not aggressive. She will need a heavy dose of confidence in order to engage in the assertive- ness strategies presented in this book. Try to boost your child's self-confidence by expressing your confidence in her. Give her encouragement and hope by telling her that the bullying can be reduced and stopped. Tell her you are optimistic that the bully- ing will stop and that she will get over the experience of being bullied. You may want to share with her the fact that a lot of famous, successful people were bullied as children—for example, Tom Cruise, Kevin Costner, Mel Gibson, Harrison Ford, Sandra Bullock, Michelle Pfeiffer, and Christina Aguilera.

Don't promise that you will not tell anyone. Promise that you will handle the situation in a way that will not make it worse. Tell her you would like to work with her to discover solutions to the problem and that it has been proven over and over that when adults get involved, bullying can be prevented and stopped. Convince her that she is not alone in the situation and is not expected to deal with it alone.

Address What Might Have Brought on the Bullying

Consider the possibility that your child may be inadvertently contributing to her mistreatment. Ask yourself, "Is my child doing something or wearing something that might be encouraging mistreatment?" For example, is she bossy, irritating, hot tempered, always interrupting others, or too aggressive? Does she have behavioral characteristics that make it more difficult for her to be accepted? No one deserves to be bullied, but sometimes there are changes that the victim needs to make. Regardless of your child's behavior, don't tolerate others blaming your child. Work with your child's teacher and others to address your child's behavior. But also ask that the school implement a program that changes the thinking, attitudes, and behavior of those around your child.

Examine your family and home environment. Is there anything happening in the family—such as spousal abuse, child abuse, divorce, and so on—that might cause your child to act out her frustration through inappropriate behavior that contributes to her lack of peer acceptance? Are any of the siblings bullying your child? Sometimes children are bullied at home, so they go to school and act out their anger through aggression—which hinders peer acceptance. Some victims at school are victims at home.

Ask yourself, "Does my child have a physical attribute that sets her apart from others?" It is sad, but our society has taught everyone to value certain physical characteristics and to devalue others. In fact, society has taught us to label some physical characteristics (such as a big nose or short stature) as "abnormal." These attitudes are wrong, but they exist. There are some characteristics that can be changed and others that cannot. For example, your child may have a scar that can be removed through cosmetic surgery. However, you cannot change your child's height. After discussing it with your child, determine if changing your child's appearance is feasible and desirable. If the changes require surgery, determine the best time and the least stigmatizing strategy for getting it done. For example, if your child must wear bandages after the surgery, it may be best to have it done in the summer.

Work with the School

Check to see if the school system has a written anti-bullying policy that the bully may be violating. If it does, then find out how to report the incident. The school should deal with all bullying incidents according to the policy. If the school doesn't have a policy and a response plan, encourage the administration to develop them. If the school's existing policy is not helpful, then try to get school leaders to improve it.

If bullying is occurring in a specific class, it is best to talk to that teacher, if you and your child feel comfortable doing so. If your child has more than one teacher, select the teacher you and your child feel most comfortable talking to. Make an appointment with your child's teacher, either by calling or e-mailing the teacher. If you don't have the teacher's e-mail address, you may be able to reach her through the school's web site or the school office. Most of the time, it is difficult to reach a teacher immediately.

When you make contact, briefly explain why you wish to meet with her. If you wish, you could briefly describe what is happening, when and where it is happening, who is involved, and who the witnesses are. Then you could suggest that she investigate the accuracy of your findings. Try not to say things that might make her defensive. For example, do not express concerns about her ability to control the students. You want to be able to collaborate with the teacher, so try to create a working relationship with her. Give her time to prepare for the meeting.

Try not to go to the school during school hours. Students will see you and may know why you are there; they may tease your child because they saw you at school. Bring a written report that you create from your bullying log. The report will give the teacher specific information about the nature and scope of the problem and motivate the school system to take action. Some experts recommend taking your child with you to the meeting. Take notes during the meeting. You may also wish to have a tape recorder in the car so that you can immediately record your mental notes after the meeting regarding the conversations and any agreements made.

At the meeting, review your child's situation and what you have discovered through your investigation. Do not exaggerate. Discuss who is involved; what has happened; the dates, times, and locations of the events; who *seems* to be the bully or bullies; who are witnesses, and so on. Explain your understanding that some of the information may need to be confirmed and the accuracy checked. Also be sure to describe how the mistreatment is affecting your child, including her physical and mental health as well as her academic performance. Then make it very clear that you want the mistreatment to stop and that you want the school to do all that it can to prevent the bullying in the future. Ask the teacher for suggestions and ideas. Be sure to give her time to talk. At this point, she may not be able to explain what is happening, but at least you have made her aware of the problem. Ask for a commitment to start or continue an investigation and to take some immediate steps to keep your child safe. Then give the teacher a couple of working days to complete her investigation. If you wish, schedule a follow-up meeting to develop a plan of action. In order to develop a comprehensive plan, the teacher may want to involve others (such as a counselor, school resource officer, or assistant principal). Tell the teacher you will e-mail her or call her in two days to review her progress. When the meeting is over, thank her for taking time to meet with you. If she has made the aforementioned commitments, thank her for agreeing to take immediate action to insure the safety of your child and for agreeing to continue her investigation.

After the meeting, send a letter to the teacher thanking her again for cooperating. The letter should also list the agreed-on actions to be taken and the date and time of the follow-up meeting to develop a plan of action. Also thank the teacher for agreeing to continue her investigation and tell her that you plan to contact her in two days. If you wish, send a copy of the letter to the principal. However, make sure you are complimentary of the teacher's professionalism, sensitivity, and concern if this seems appropriate.

Most teachers will be cooperative. However, if the teacher is not cooperative, you and your child and, if appropriate, other victimized students and their parents should go to the teacher's supervisor (in other words, the principal). Most principals will be helpful, but you may find one who denies that bullying is an issue in the school or who just wants to blame your child. For example, she might say, "We have really good kids here. I don't think bullying is a problem here." Or she might say, "You know, your child isn't liked here. Maybe you need to consider transferring your child." When you find a principal like this, be wary, but meet with her anyway. Once again, make sure you have your facts at hand. At the meeting, explain exactly what you told the teacher and ask the principal to tell you when she plans to talk to the person who is bullying your child and to your child's teacher. Following the meeting, call the principal to see if the meetings occurred. The principal is not required to tell you what action was taken with the bully. In fact, that could be a violation of the bully's privacy rights. If action has not been taken or you are not satisfied with the principal's response, tell her that you plan to go to the next level (the superintendent) and that if necessary, you will go to the board of education.

Call the superintendent and tell her that your child is being hurt, so her prompt action is important. Ask for a meeting. Make sure you have gathered all the facts and have a record of your meetings. If the superintendent is not cooperative or seems to be refusing to meet with you, contact the chair of the board of education or another board member you trust.

If the teacher is making an effort but seems to be unable to help your child, even after two or three revisions of the plan of action, schedule a meeting with the principal. Explain that the teacher has been professional and cooperative, but needs some assistance. Also explain that the mistreatment has continued far too long and that you are concerned about the impact it is having on your child. Explain that it is time for the school to step up its efforts. Ask the principal to make a commitment to take action and to recommend the next steps. If you agree on the steps, ask for a time frame in which they will be implemented. Then schedule a follow-up meeting with the principal to discuss the effectiveness of the implementation and what should be done next.

One parent had the principal call a meeting of the victim and the bullies. The principal and the parent of the victim also attended the meeting. At the meeting, the victim asked the bullies to explain their behavior. The principal warned the bullies that they would be suspended if they mistreated the girl again, and the behavior stopped. Confronting the bullies and communicating that there will be serious consequences for bullying are sometimes effective in stopping the behavior. However, just warning or just talking to the bullies about their behavior is not as effective as applying negative consequences and rewarding appropriate behavior.

As strategies are implemented, schedule follow-up appointments with the appropriate school personnel to assess whether action taken by the school has been successful. Try to be patient;

bullying is a difficult problem to solve. However, expect action to be taken by the school in a timely manner. Seriously consider any suggestions school personnel give you. Also ask that there be an adult (that is, a support teacher) to whom your child can talk every day to give an update on her mistreatment.

If you are not satisfied with the response of the school system, you may want to talk to an attorney to see what rights your child has and if any action can be taken. You'll have to decide if you want your child in the school under those conditions, but sometimes a letter from an attorney is all that is needed. You might be able to ask the school system to assign your child to a different teacher or even a different school. You might also want to talk to your attorney to see if your child can legally take a small tape or video recorder to school and record the mistreatment. (You don't want to get into trouble for tape recording someone without permission.) There are recorders about the size of your little finger. Some parents of victims have obtained a restraining order against bullies. The bullies had to stay so many feet away from their child, and the school had to ensure that the order was enforced. You can also consider filing assault charges against the bully. Talk to the police or an attorney about the different types of assault charges.

Ask your child's school system and school to implement an anti-bullying program and to make sure school personnel are trained to prevent and stop bullying. Offer your assistance. Ask them to visit www.bullyfree.com. All school personnel need to know how to create schools where all students feel accepted and have a sense of belonging. They also need to learn how to prevent and stop bullying, how to help victims, and how to change bullies. Ask local parent organizations, civic organizations, or corporations to sponsor an anti-bullying workshop or seminar. Teachers also need bullying prevention curriculum materials and anti-bullying campaign resources (brochures, bracelets, and posters).

Determine if there is anti-bullying legislation in your state. It may be that your child's school system has a legislative responsibility to have an anti-bullying policy, program, or both. If your state doesn't have such legislation, there are probably agencies in your state that can help you try to get such legislation passed.

Promote anti-bullying activities through local PTAs (or PTOs). Ask that bullying be placed on the agenda of a meeting and that a guest speaker be invited to address bullying.

Report All Threats and Physical Assaults

Any physical assaults or threats should be taken very seriously. Take pictures of all injuries and hold a ruler next to the injuries to show their sizes; keep a record of all medical treatment, all medical expenses, and all related travel expenses, including counseling. Date the pictures and code them in a way that links them to notes in your log about the specific bullying event that caused the injuries.

Report all physical assaults to the school and to the police. Going to the police is a serious step, but where there is serious harassment or a serious assault, it is an important one. In such situations, insist that the police make out a charge sheet. This will make your child feel better and may deter the bully. However, keep in mind that police action sometimes has its drawbacks and can call unwanted attention to your child or, conversely, cause them to be shunned.

You could also encourage parents of other victimized children to contact the police. Perhaps if more parents contacted the police, more children would get the message that bullying will not be tolerated. I had one principal tell me that he just about stopped bullying in his school by calling the police every time he had a problem with bullies. The police would go to the school and interview the bully in the presence of an adult and take whatever action was appropriate. He said that explaining the possible legal consequences of the behavior was all it took. I'm not necessarily recommending this approach for every situation, but it can be an effective strategy for getting the no-bullying message across to kids. The truth is that by contacting the police, some parents have saved the lives of their children or saved them from serious injury. Some children have had bones broken, an eye damaged, and even brain damage from beatings by bullies. Personally, if I felt my child's life were threatened or that there were a likelihood of serious injury, I would not hesitate to call the police.

Because laws vary from state to state, the response of the police may vary. In some states, children seventeen and over are considered adults, and the law is applied accordingly. Usually, children fourteen to seventeen are charged and judged in a children's court. Children younger than fourteen usually are not charged unless the incident is serious, but the police can still interview the child in the presence of an adult, and can make certain demands.

Police are used to dealing with assault or harassment complaints and can be helpful. However, there have been reports of cases in which the police said there was nothing they could do, when in fact they could have at least recommended other options made possible by laws of their state, such as filing a complaint with a worker designated by the district court. In some states, the police may recommend that you talk to an officer of a special juvenile division or unit. An officer of the unit will probably ask to speak to your child in your presence or in the presence of another adult. She may also ask to see the facts you have written down and any pictures you have taken of the injuries. If you have taken your child to a doctor because of the injuries received, the officer will ask for a copy of the doctor's report. Ask her to send a copy of the interview transcript to your attorney.

When School Personnel Bully

When you have a problem with an adult who works at your child's school, you should go directly to her first and share the facts that you have recorded. Try to think positively of her first and assume she might be cooperative. Of course, sometimes you will be disappointed. Be open minded—perhaps she doesn't realize how hurtful she is being. If her behavior is injuring your child physically, emotionally, psychologically, or socially, you need to let her know immediately. Be sure to take good notes on the conversation at the meeting. You might also want to have a tape recorder available so you can record your thoughts on what was said or to take someone with you to the meeting to confirm what was said. If the adult is mistreating other students, ask those students and their parents to go with you.

If the adult is not cooperative, you and your child, as well as the other victimized students and their parents, should go to the person's supervisor (the principal). If you are not satisfied with the supervisor's response, you should tell her that you plan to go to the next level (the superintendent). If necessary, you may have to go to the chair of the board of education or someone on the board you respect and trust. Make sure you have your facts in order. Of course, other victimized students and their parents can go with you to each of the meetings.

Find out what other parents and students know about the adult. When you talk to them, don't mention your child's bullying situation. Seek information in an informal way and don't criticize the person.

Check to see if the school system has any written personnel policies that the adult is violating by mistreating your child. There may be a harassment policy that addresses personnel mistreating others. If such a policy does exist, ask the school to enforce the policy.

If you are not satisfied with the response of the school system, you may want to talk to an attorney to see if any action can be taken. Sometimes a letter from an attorney is all that is needed. You may want to ask the school system to change your child's schedule so that the individual can be avoided as much as possible, or ask to have your child assigned to a different school. You might also want to talk to your attorney and see if your child can legally take a small tape recorder or video camera to school and record the mistreatment.

Identify Early Signs of Traumatic Stress

Watch for signs of depression in your child, and do not hesitate to seek professional counseling for her. School guidance counselors can be helpful, but many times the school counselor doesn't have the time to give your child the attention she needs. If you are a member of a religious organization, you might consider seeking pastoral counseling for your child. If you decide to send her to a professional counselor, try to prepare your child for the first meeting. Review the situation with her: What has happened? How often does the mistreatment happen? How long has the mistreatment been going on? When and where does it happen? Who is involved? What do the bystanders do? How do you feel about what is happening? Does it make you feel sick? What do you think should be done? Who are the adults you feel could help you?

Depression in children and adolescents is not uncommon. Children who experience repeated mistreatment are at risk of becoming depressed. The depression creates a vicious cycle for them. Among both children and adolescents, depressive disorders can increase their risk for illness and interpersonal and psychosocial difficulties that persist long after the depressive episode is resolved; in adolescents there is also an increased risk for substance abuse and suicidal behavior. Unfortunately, these disorders often go unrecognized by families and physicians alike. Signs of depressive disorders in young people often are viewed as normal mood swings typical of a particular developmental stage. In addition, health care professionals may be reluctant to prematurely label a young person with a mental illness diagnosis. Yet early diagnosis and treatment of depressive disorders are critical to healthy emotional, social, and behavioral development. For more information on depressive disorders, see the mental health resources listed in Appendix B.

Because being bullied can be traumatic for some children, watch for signs of posttraumatic stress disorder (PTSD). It has only recently been understood that bullying may cause PTSD in some children and adolescents. According to the National Center for Posttraumatic Stress Disorder, PTSD is a psychiatric disorder that can occur following the experience or witnessing of life-threatening events, such as military combat; natural disasters; terrorist incidents; serious accidents; violent personal assaults, such as rape; and persistent mistreatment, such as physical abuse and bullying.[3] People who suffer from PTSD often relive the experience through nightmares and flashbacks, have difficulty sleeping, and feel detached or estranged. These symptoms can be severe enough and last long enough to significantly impair the person's daily life. PTSD is marked by clear biological changes as well as psychological symptoms. It is complicated by the fact that it frequently occurs in conjunction with related disorders, such as depression, substance abuse, problems of memory and cognition, and other problems of physical and mental health. The disorder is also associated with impairment of the person's ability to function in social or family life, including occupational instability, marital problems and divorces, family discord, and difficulties in parenting.

When you examine the national center's list of characteristics of individuals who are most likely to develop PTSD, you can clearly see why some bullying victims develop the disorder.

Individuals at Increased Risk for PTSD

- Those who experience greater stressor magnitude and intensity, unpredictability, uncontrollability, sexual (as opposed to nonsexual) victimization, real or perceived responsibility, and betrayal

- Those with prior vulnerability factors, such as genetics, early age of onset and longer-lasting childhood trauma, lack of functional social support, and concurrent stressful life events

- Those who report greater perceived threat or danger, suffering, terror and horror, or fear

- Those with a social environment that produces shame, guilt, stigmatization, or self-hatred

If you suspect that your child has PTSD, seek professional counseling for her.

Watch for signs that your child may be suicidal. Children who are persistently mistreated and experience depression for a significant amount of time may have suicidal thoughts. Depression in children and adolescents is associated with an increased risk of suicidal behaviors. This risk may rise, particularly among adolescent boys, if the depression is accompanied by a conduct disorder and alcohol or other substance abuse. In 1997, suicide was the third leading cause of death in ten- to twenty-four-year-olds. Research supported by the National Institute of Mental Health found that among adolescents who develop major depressive disorders, as many as 7 percent may commit suicide in the young adult years.[1] Consequently, it is important for doctors and parents to take all threats of suicide seriously.

Researchers are developing and testing various interventions to prevent suicide in children and adolescents. Early diagnosis and treatment, accurate evaluation of suicidal thinking, and limiting young people's access to lethal agents—including firearms and medications—may hold the greatest suicide prevention value.

The American Academy of Experts in Traumatic Stress emphasizes that discussing the possibility of suicide with your child does not increase the likelihood that she will commit suicide. The academy recommends seeking answers to the following questions:[5]

- Have you been feeling depressed? (Adjust language depending on age—"sad," "bummed-out," or "blue.")
- How long have you been feeling depressed?
- Do you feel that everything is hopeless?
- Have you experienced difficulty sleeping (for example, trouble falling asleep or middle-of-night awakening)?

- Has your appetite changed? (For example, have you gained or lost weight?)

- Have you found yourself turning to alcohol or other substances to help you cope?

- During this time, have you ever had thoughts of killing yourself?

- When did these thoughts occur?

- What did you think about doing to yourself?

- Did you act on your thoughts?

- What stopped you from doing it?

- How often have these thoughts occurred?

- When was the last time you had these thoughts?

- Can you promise that you will not harm yourself?

- Have your thoughts ever included harming someone else in addition to yourself?

- How often has that occurred?

- What have you thought about doing to the other person or people?

- Have you taken any steps toward acquiring a gun, pills, and so on?

- Have you thought about the effect that your death would have on your family or friends?

- What help could make it easier for you to cope with your current thoughts and plans?

- What makes you want to live?

- How does talking about this make you feel?

A child who desires to end her life needs immediate attention. Individuals who are actively suicidal often have multiple signs of distress. These signs may include the following:

- Saying farewell to peers
- Giving away prized possessions
- Writing essays or notes about suicide
- Verbalizing to a peer or teacher about "not wanting to be around any longer"
- Excessive fatigue
- Sudden changes in personality
- Self-destructive behavior (such as self-mutilation)

When a child has suicidal thoughts or actually makes an attempt, there are a number of things you can do. For example, if your child says she wants to die, take it seriously and have a heart-to-heart talk with her. Do not assume that she doesn't really mean it. Talking about it will not make her commit suicide. Always leave the door open for such discussion in the future, especially when the child expresses her feelings about traumatic events or stressors of life. If your child talks about suicide or has attempted suicide, get professional help. If she has made a serious attempt, she probably needs to go directly to a hospital. Once her medical needs have been met, she needs to see a psychiatrist. If your child makes a suicide attempt or has a plan, do not leave her alone until she has been assessed, which could take one or more days. This can be exhausting, so make sure also to take care of yourself while you help your child. Also make sure that she doesn't have access to methods of suicide, such as medications, guns, ropes, razors, and so on. Lock these items up or get them out of the house.

Some children use suicidal thoughts and attempts as a means of manipulating or hurting others, even to get out of school. Although your initial reaction should always be to take your child seriously, you should also keep this possibility in mind and work with your child's therapist to find the root cause of the suicidal feelings.

What Else Can You Do to Help?

Identify caring school personnel who are willing to help your child—perhaps even befriend her. This may be a teacher or staff member you know well who works in your child's school. Ask her to monitor your child's interactions with others and to talk frequently with your child.

Involve your child in activities inside and outside school. Help her make friends with new children who can help break the cycle of mistreatment. For example, your child might become a scout or join a club or youth group in a local church. Your child could also have an e-mail friend or pen pal—with your supervision.

Monitor your child's whereabouts and her friendships. If your child feels rejected, she may seek friendships with the wrong people in the wrong places. The need to have a sense of belonging and acceptance is so strong that if it is not met with peers with good morals, your child may seek to make friends with individuals who have trouble distinguishing right from wrong. Some children will join gangs, hate groups, cults, and drug groups in order to have a place to belong and to feel safer.

Help your child establish a meaningful relationship with her grandparents and other members of her extended family. This will broaden the support network for your child.

Read books about bullying with your child. Discuss the bullying situations described in these books and other content relevant to bullying. Be careful when purchasing children's books about bullying. Some of them send the wrong message. Sometimes they place too much emphasis on empathy for the bully or even promote retaliation. Therefore, as you read such books, be discerning. If you feel uncomfortable with the messages communicated by the stories, share your thoughts with your child. I recommend that you search the Internet to learn as much as you can about anti-bullying books before you purchase them or read them with your child. Before you purchase such books, see if you can check them out at your local or nearby college or university library. A few children's books that I would recommend are listed here.

Help your child deal with the fear that she feels. Do not minimize it, but don't overreact. Demonstrate how to control fear. Assess those things that are making her fearful to determine whether action needs to be taken. Managing fear is important for two reasons. If she is fearful, which is a normal response to bullying, she is more likely to become an easy target: she will look fearful. Bullies often target fearful people. Give your child the following tips for coping with fear:

- Accept fearful feelings as a normal response and don't be afraid to feel them. Don't deny you are fearful, don't try to hide it, don't pretend that you are not fearful, and don't seek to do something wrong (such as skipping school) to avoid the fear.

- Express your fear in an appropriate manner. Talk to your parents about your fearful feelings, write a letter to your parents about your fear, write about it in your journal, draw pictures about it, or write a song or poem about it.

- Accept fear as a challenge. See it as something you can conquer. It provides an opportunity for you to be a winner—a winner over your fear and the things that make you fearful.

- Bottle your fears inside of a bottle, not inside of you. Every night and every morning, imagine yourself placing all of your fears in a bottle and screwing on the top.

- Keep a small smooth pretty stone in your pocket. When someone or something makes you fearful, place your hand in your pocket and feel of the beautiful rock as a reminder to relax.

- Learn to use breathing to help you control fear. Start by standing or sitting straight, then breathe through your nose. When you breathe in, your stomach should go out and you should feel your lungs filling up with air. Make your breathing a little longer than normal. Hold your breath until you count to three, and then let it out slowly while pulling your stomach in.

- Tense and relax your muscles.

- Do not exaggerate the fear. Sometimes we think about what might happen, rather than what is actually happening. Try to think only about what is currently happening.

- Try to imagine the people and situations that make you fearful and then visualize yourself being calm, smiling, and walking off. Imagine the person making you fearful sitting in front of you in a chair and telling them over and over, "You cannot make me fearful. I will not let you make me fearful."

ANTI-BULLYING BOOKS FOR CHILDREN

AGES 2–5

I'll Fix Anthony, *by Judith Viorst*

No Regard Beauregard and the Golden Rule, *by James Rice*

Swimmy, *by Leo Lionni*

Why Are You Mean to Me? *by Deborah Hautig*

AGES 3–8

Abby's Wish, *by Liza St. John*

Best Enemies, *by Kathleen Leverich*

Goggles! *by Ezra Jack Keats*

King of the Playground, *by Phyllis Reynolds Naylor*

Pinky and Rex and the Bully, *by James Howe*

Stop Picking on Me, *by Pat Thomas and Lesley Harber*

Tyrone the Horrible, *by Hans Wilheim*

The Very Bad Bunny, *by Marilyn Sadler*

AGES 9–14

Bad Girls, *by Cynthia Voigt*

Karen's Bully, *by Ann Martin*

Flip Flop Girl, *by Katherine Paterson*

Fourth Grade Rats, *by Jerry Spinelli*

How You Can Be Bully Free (Grades 4–8), *by Allan L. Beane*

Present Takers, *by Aidan Chambers*

The Best School Year Ever, *by Barbara Robinson*

The Boy Who Lost His Face, *by Louis Sachar*

The Meanest Thing to Say, *by Bill Cosby*

Stick Up for Yourself, *by Gershen Kaufman*

AGES 15 AND UP

Dear Mr. Henshaw, *by Beverly Cleary*

How You Can Be Bully Free (Grades 9–12), *by Allan L. Beane*

The Diddakoi, *by Rumer Golden*

Several videos are available to help you develop character traits you desire in your child; some videos deal specifically with bullying. Search the Internet for titles and availability. Unfortunately, videos can be very expensive. Before you purchase any, see if you can check them out at your local library or nearby college or university library. Be sure to preview them before viewing them with your child.

Involve your child in discovering solutions to her bullying situation. Ask your child what she thinks should be done to stop the mistreatment. She may offer good suggestions. With your help, your child may be able to diffuse the problem herself.

Be aware of signs that your child is bullying her siblings. Children who are victims at school sometimes bully their siblings. They don't want to be victimized at school and at home, so they strike out at family members. Sometimes this behavior is an expression of anger created by being a victim. Talk to your child about any bullying behavior you see in her and explain that although you understand where it comes from, it has to stop.

Be an observant parent. Listen to what your child says and what others are saying to your child. Also watch your child interacting with others.

Your child will need to be as physically fit as possible to deal with the stress caused by bullying. So make sure she gets a good night's sleep, exercises regularly, and eats the right foods. Sleep is especially important. Lack of sleep affects impulse control and can impact your child's interactions with others, as well as her ability to cope with bullying.

Ask an older student with good morals to mentor your child. Mentoring can be effective, as mentors share wisdom gained from personal experience. The mentor can go places with your child and do a lot of fun things with her.

If necessary, transfer your child to another school or school system. Your child may need a "fresh start." This strategy is not always effective, but it could give her a chance to leave all the labels behind and have a new beginning. It is better to transfer a child at the beginning of the school year than after school has already started. Another alternative is to homeschool your child. If the school can do nothing to prevent the bullying situations, then it is better to remove your child than to let bullying take its toll on her self-esteem, physical and emotional health, and social development. If you don't transfer your child and the bullying continues, your child may feel that the school cannot meet her needs and may resent that the school has not stopped the bullying. This could cause her to build up anger toward you and toward school personnel, leading to disrespect and discipline problems.

When you see or hear about your child effectively coping with bullying, reward her verbally and with a special privilege or treat. In other words, reward her survivor behavior.

Discuss the bullying with other parents of children who have been bullied. They may share ways they have helped their own children and how their children have been able to cope with or end the bullying they experienced.

Don't give up. Most school personnel are supportive and want to help. However, you may find a few who seem to ignore you or brush you off. Don't let them do that to you. Don't feel as though you are being a troublemaker or that you are taking up too much of their time. Your child's safety and health must be a priority. By stopping bullying, you are helping your child, other children, and the school.

Maintain open lines of communication with your child. Ask her to keep you posted on her mistreatment. When the time feels right, conversationally ask probing questions to determine if there are improvements in her situation.

Keep telling your child that you love her. Hug her a lot and give her your time and attention. Be approachable, courteous, considerate, and respectful. Be willing to defer something you want to do in order to do what she wants. In other words, go out of your way to be good to her and to communicate that she is important to you. Your love for her will help her love herself and accept herself. Self-acceptance is the basis for self-improvement, and self-love is the basis for compassion toward others.

KEY MESSAGES

- Be thankful that you know your child is being bullied.

- Stay calm even though you are concerned.

- Avoid being a "fix-it" parent who immediately calls the bully's parents.

- Don't tell your child to retaliate.

- No matter how minor the event seems to be, take it seriously.

- Ask questions to find out what happened.

- Keep a log of the bullying events.

- Give your child tips on how to respond to the bullying.

- If the bullying is happening in the school, meet with school personnel and collaborate with them to help your child.

- Teach your child to be assertive.

- Report all physical assaults to the school and police.

- Promote the establishment of an anti-bullying program in your child's school.

7

Preventing Cyberbullying

Dear Dr. Beane:

I just wanted to contact you about my son's experiences. I know you know from first-hand experience, through your son, how destructive bullying can be. I was not aware that my son was being bullied for several years. I was always concerned about him. He seemed to be getting sadder and sadder and was withdrawing from the friends he did have. I was finally told about the bullying by one of his friends. But it was too late. My son had already committed suicide. Students were so mean to my son. I was told that the most recent thing they did to him was to post a lot of mean ugly things on the Internet about him. It appears that when they started using computers to hurt my son, it was more than he could handle.

You and your child need to know how to handle a new form of bullying—cyberbullying, or electronic bullying. According to Bill Belsey, president of Bullying.org (Canada), "Cyberbullying involves the use of information and communication technologies such as email, cell phone and pager text messages, instant messaging, defamatory personal web sites, and defamatory online personal polling web sites to support deliberate, repeated, and hostile behaviour by an individual or group, that is intended to harm others."[1]

Cyberbullying is becoming more and more popular because with just a few strokes on the computer keyboard, hurtful and destructive information can be anonymously sent to or posted for viewing by thousands of people. Cyberbullying intensifies the victim's feelings that there is no escape. It can thus be even more destructive and hurtful than other forms of bullying.[2] The consequences for those cyberbullied are devastating. When cyberbullying caps off years of mistreatment, some victims become depressed and suicidal.[3]

What Does Cyberbullying Look Like?

Cyberbullying comes in a variety of forms. Children are discovering more and more creative ways to use technology to hurt people. The attacks can be direct or by proxy. Cyberbullying by proxy occurs when a cyberbully gets someone else to do the bullying. Most of the time, this person does not know that he is being used by the cyberbully.[4] This is the most dangerous form of cyberbullying because it can get adults involved in the bullying who are unaware that they are dealing with a child. Sometimes cyberbullies attack by posing as the victim to create problems for the true victim. For example, the bully may make it look as though the victim is doing something wrong; the parents are then notified, and the parents punish the victim. Some examples of cyberbullying include using technology to

- Spread malicious gossip, rumors, and lies
- Post defamatory photographs and video recordings on the web
- Send mean, nasty, and ugly e-mails
- Send malicious code
- Send porn and other junk e-mails and instant messages (IMs)
- Impersonate the victim
- Send cruel jokes

- Send or post embarrassing information or photographs
- Create web sites designed to humiliate and embarrass someone

A cyberbully might also use one or more of the following online forums to bully your child. You need to be familiar with these so that you can help your child:[5]

- *Blogs (web logs)*. Blogs provide users with the tools to publish personal content online about a range of topics, such as hobbies, travel, or work projects. People then connect their blogs with those of other people with similar interests.
- *Chat rooms*. These are virtual meeting places where users can find people to talk with online. Most chat rooms can accommodate more than one hundred users simultaneously.
- *Discussion groups (newsgroups)*. Discussion groups are accessible via the Internet. Each group (forum) is categorized and devoted to a single topic. Messages are posted in bulletin form and remain on a server, rather than being e-mailed.
- *E-mail (electronic mail)*. E-mail is a service that allows subscribers to pass messages from one person to the other through an Internet service provider (ISP).
- *Instant messaging (IM)*. This is an online activity that allows two or more people to converse online. Subscribers can create a contact list of those with whom they want to communicate.
- *Message boards*. These are online places where people with common interests go to talk about those interests, such as sports teams, TV shows, and online games.
- *Short message service (SMS)*. This is a service that allows text messages to be sent and received via cell phones.

What Are Warning Signs That Your Child Is Being Cyberbullied?

The warning signs presented in Chapter Two also apply to cyberbullying. If you suspect that your child is being cyberbullied, review those signs and ask yourself whether your child

- Has large cell phone charges from the same telephone number
- Spends long hours on the computer using chat rooms
- Visits web sites that promote nasty rumors, such as schoolscandals.com
- Seems to be upset, irritable, or emotional after spending time on the computer
- Talks about pictures of him on the Internet that were posted without permission
- Seems to be secretive about use of the computer
- Sends or receives e-mail messages that use symbols and codes

What You Can Do

Protecting your child from all cyberbullying may be impossible. But there are some steps you can take to prevent much of it, reduce it, and perhaps even stop some cyberbullies.

First, make sure that your child knows what cyberbullying is and what it looks like. Discuss how students use technology to mistreat and hurt people. Ask your child if he knows anyone who has been cyberbullied. Ask your child to give you some examples of cyberbullying and then you can provide a few yourself.

Tell your child that it is important that you have open lines of communication with one another. No matter how insignificant the hurtful actions of others may seem to be to your child, you want to know about them. When it comes to mistreatment, there are no secrets.

Make it your business to know what your child is doing through his computer and cell phone. Explain to your child that as a parent you have a moral and legal obligation to protect him, and you have the legal right to search his computer and examine his cell phone, regardless of whether or not he purchased it with his own money. Whenever you feel you need to examine his communication devices to better protect him, do so.

Develop your computer skills so that you can keep track of your child's Internet activities and can visit the sites your child is visiting. Because many cyberbullies use a cyber language, online lingo, or Internet slang, this can make it difficult for parents to understand what is being said. Learn some of the common shortcuts for words and phrases that are used in texting, e-mails, and chat rooms. The following are some examples of shortcuts you should be aware of:

ADN: any day now

A/S/L: age, sex, location

BF: boyfriend

BYAM: between you and me

F2F: face to face

GF: girlfriend

KPC: keeping parents clueless

IWSN: I want sex now

NIFOC: nude in front of computer

PIR: parent in room

POS: parent over shoulder

TDTM: talk dirty to me

YBS: you'll be sorry

Visit http://en.wikipedia.org/wiki/Internet_slang for an exhaustive and growing catalog of Internet slang.

Let your child know that you have the same skills and ability to engage in the same activities he does over the computer. Also learn as much as you can about cell phones and the different ways information can be communicated and shared.

Some forms of cyberbullying can be dealt with in much the same way that you deal with other forms of bullying. For example, written assertive comments may prove to be effective. However, it is important for your child not to write anything that provokes the bully or that could be used against him if legal action were ever pursued. Therefore, you may prefer to tell your child to ignore the bully. Select other response strategies mentioned in this book that seem to be most appropriate for your child and the cyberbullying. Keep in mind that not all strategies work in every situation for all children, but they are worth a try. You yourself could also send a clear message to the bully: "Do not contact or communicate with my child anymore or we will contact the appropriate authorities." But do not be surprised if the cyberbullying doesn't stop.

If it continues, gather information and documentation and determine the facts. Print and save documents that verify that your child is being cyberbullied. For example, ask your child to report to you cyberbullying messages and to print the messages. Tell your child that such messages are unlawful. Report the messages to the police and to your ISP and provide the necessary proof.

Decide if it is a good idea to contact the parents of the cyberbullies. They may be parents who will not tolerate such behavior and will be surprised to hear that their child is engaged in it. Unfortunately, sometimes the parents of cyberbullies get defensive. Therefore, consider not meeting them face-to-face but instead sending them a certified letter that includes the downloaded material and requests that the cyberbullying stop and all harmful material be removed.[6]

Teach your child that the Golden Rule also applies when using technology. If your child mistreats others, he is likely get the same kind of treatment. Being polite, kind, and encouraging to others usually has positive results. Therefore, it is best not to send messages when one is upset or angry. Explain that you will not tolerate your child participating cyberbullying himself. Tell your child that using the computer is a privilege and that a privilege can be limited or even lost if it is not used in an acceptable manner. Then give him a set of rules. The following are some examples:

Cyber Rules

- Never give out personal contact information about yourself, your parents, or your friends—such as a name, address, phone number, age, or e-mail address—without a parent's permission.

- Never give out intimate personal information or personal interest information that should be discussed only with parents, family, close friends, or professionals.

- Never give out any passwords to anyone other than parents.

- Never use inappropriate language, and never write anything that you wouldn't mind the world reading.

- Treat others online the way you want to be treated.

- Immediately report any hurtful comments and threats against yourself or anyone else, and stop communicating.

- Do not participate in gossip or spreading rumors—stop communicating.

- Time on the Internet and e-mail is limited to _____ per day, except when completing homework.

- Never upload or download pictures, music, or videos without a parent's permission.

Also consider limiting the amount of time your child spends on the computer sending messages and visiting web sites that are used to communicate or post information. The more time your child spends responding to the comments of others, the more likely it is that he might say something about someone that gets back to that person. It is difficult for children not to respond to derogatory comments about others.

Frequently monitor your child's use of the computer. Do not put a computer in your child's room where he can shut the door and you are unable to see the screen. Locate it in a place where you can easily monitor and supervise its use. You should be able to walk by and see what your child is working on. Some parents have placed the computer where there is a lot of traffic in the house, making it easy to look over the shoulder of their child. Laptop computers have made it possible for computers to be used in any room in the house and could make monitoring easier.

You have the right to make specific web sites off-limits for your child. Make a list of the web sites your child cannot visit. Explain that the list is not exhaustive and will be updated. Of course, you should make it clear that he cannot visit any web sites that promote hate, violence, racism, and pornography, as well as web sites that use profanity and sexual language. You may wish to purchase tracking or blocking software to track web sites visited by your child. If you do, tell your child what you are doing to regulate his use of the Internet. You can purchase a blocking software program that will block out messages and sites that contain content related to sex, violence, racism, and profanity. Some of the most popular programs are CyberSitter, Cyber Patrol, Net Nanny, and Surfwatch.

If your child is being bullied online, also consider software that helps discover the identity of the bullies, such as Email Tracker Pro, McAfee Parental Controls, and Security Soft's Predator Guard. Such programs offer filtering protection and scan for inappropriate text, even threatening and harassing content. I can't testify to the effectiveness of these programs, but they may be of some help. Never rely completely on technology to protect your child, however. Always combine it with supervision and discussions with your child about appropriate use of the Internet.

Limit the number of people to whom you give your or your child's e-mail addresses and phone numbers. Tell your child never to give out personal information, including e-mail addresses, telephone numbers, home address, pictures, personal video recordings, user ID or password, or credit card information, especially to strangers or someone he met online. Do not hesitate to change e-mail addresses and cell phone numbers if they are being used to harass or bully your child.

Teach your child not to believe everything he reads on the Internet. People often spread rumors and lies to hurt others. The best thing for your child to do when he sees these comments is to log off. Tell him not to respond to the statements.

If your child receives threats, make sure he knows that threats should be viewed as serious. Tell him not to delete the message, but to print it. Give a copy to law enforcement officials. Also show the message to an attorney. This is discussed later in this chapter.

Tell your child always to play it safe. For example, if the sender's name and address are unfamiliar, don't open a message or any attachments and do not respond to the message. Ask your child to report these messages to you so you can record or print the information. Also tell your child to trust his instincts. If a message doesn't look right or feel right, it probably isn't.

Tell your child not to interact with bullies in any way through a cell phone or computer. He should not respond to the bullies, no matter how tempting it is. This is not a time to lash out at the bully. Bullies have been known to print the responses and try to get their victims into trouble. This may be a challenge for your child. Anyone would find it difficult just to ignore such messages.

If the bullying happens through a personal account, report the situation to the bully's e-mail account provider, which is usually the word after the @ sign. If your child's e-mail and IM accounts allow it, block e-mails and instant messages from the bully. Also check to see if your child's phone allows you to turn off incoming text messages; look under Help or Tools. Sometimes it is best for your child to avoid using the phone or computer (other than in approved ways) altogether for a few days to see if the bully gives up. Let the telephone take messages.

Restrict the people who can send your child communications. Consider restricting all incoming communications to pre-approved senders, such as those on your child's buddy list. Make sure the bully is not on the buddy list. Also restrict others from being able to add your child to their buddy list. This feature is usually found in the privacy settings or parental controls of a communications program.[7] Don't let your child record his own voicemail message and say his name, because these will confirm for the bully that he has the right number and will enable him to mistreat your child. Because the bully may recognize your child's voice, use the message provided by the telephone service. Tell your child this should never be changed and that you will be checking it frequently.

Some parents have also made all chat rooms off-limits. If you allow your child to use chat rooms, tell him to exit when individuals start mistreating him or someone else. Ask your child to write down the individual's screen name and report it to you. Then you should report the individual to the police, your ISP, and the administrator of the chat room. If your child really enjoys using a chat room and you agree to let him sign up again, make sure he does so with a different ID. Remind him not to provide any personal information.

File a complaint with your ISP. Even though some behaviors experienced by your child may not break the law, they could break the rules and regulations of certain ISPs, which means that your ISP may be able to help you deal with a cyberbully. If there is a web site (blog, message board, online voting site) that says bad things about your child, print it and give a copy to your ISP. Many of the popular sites have links you can click to report harassment, threats, and other forms of bullying. Some examples are listed here.[8]

REPORTING CYBERBULLYING TO SERVICE PROVIDERS

MYSPACE

To report offensive profiles and report harassment or threats, go to the help page at www.myspace.com.

FACEBOOK

Report abuse by e-mailing Facebook at privacy@facebook.com or through the Privacy page at www.facebook.com. Use the e-mail address info@facebook.com to report any other content you think should not be posted.

XANGA

Go to the Report Inappropriate Content page at http://help.xanga.com.

YOUTUBE

You can flag any video on this site as inappropriate. If YouTube reviews the video and finds it to be inappropriate, the video will be removed. For further information, go to the Code of Conduct page at http://youtube.com.

WIREDSAFETY

To access WiredSafety's online forms for severe cases of cyberbullying, go to the Report Cyberabuses page at www.wiredsafety.org.

Tell your child never to arrange a face-to-face meeting with someone he met online until you've checked out who the person is and his background. Explain that individuals can say nice things over the telephone or computer, but they could be hiding the fact that they are not nice and may even desire to hurt your child.

If cyberbullying is occurring at your child's school, contact the school. Ask the school for a copy of their anti-bullying policy, harassment policy, and cell phone use policy. Examine them for language that relates to the mistreatment of your child. Bullying is bullying. It does not matter if the bullying occurs in the hallway or bathroom or over a cell phone or the Internet at school. Encourage your child's school to include cyberbullying in its policies. It is difficult, if not impossible, for schools to discipline children for cyberbullying if it does not occur at school, on school property, or on their way home or to school. However, you should inform the school so that personnel can keep an eye on interactions with your child. Many times, cyberbullying is an extension of bullying in the school.

Reporting Cyberbullying to the Police

All forms of cyberbullying should be taken seriously. They can be destructive to the well-being of your child, causing depression, overwhelming anxiety, academic difficulties, and behavior problems. It is especially devastating when your child is also bullied at school or in other settings.

Some cyberbullying should be reported to the police. When cyberbullies threaten your child, make racist remarks, or try to ruin his reputation, they should be reported to the police. Because fewer than 30 percent of victims know their cyberbullies, they are often threatened because the anonymity empowers the attackers.[9] It is important to maintain a record of the threats. As mentioned earlier, printouts are generally not considered admissible evidence. Instead, you should use a monitoring program, such as Spectorsoft.[10] This is a software program that collects and preserves electronic evidence. However, do not install or remove any programs or take other remedial action on your computer or communication device during this process, as it may adversely affect the investigation.[11]

Taking Legal Action

You should think long and hard before you decide to take legal action. Such action can be very time consuming and costly. It could take several years and tens of thousands of dollars to bring legal action against a cyberbully.[12] Try other strategies first. The fact that you tried other alternatives will help your case if you do decide to bring legal action. Sometimes, threatening to close the cyberbully's ISP or instant messaging account is enough to make the bullying stop. However, there may be times you will want to obtain the services of a lawyer. Before taking such action, make sure you have hard evidence saved on your computer. Bill Belsey, recognized as an international expert on cyberbullying, says that the more you have saved, the easier it will be to track down the cyberbullies. He suggests that you[13]

- Save the following from e-mail:
  E-mail address
  Date and time received
  Copies of any relevant e-mails with full e-mail headers

- Save the following from groups or communities:
  URL of offending group site
  User name of offending person
  E-mail address of offending person
  Date you saw it happen

- Save the following from profiles you see on the web:
  URL of profile
  User name of offending person
  E-mail address of offending person
  Date you viewed this profile

- Save the following from chat rooms:
  Date and time of chat
  Name and URL of chat room you were in
  User name of offending person
  E-mail address of offending person
  Screenshot of chat room

Keeping Up-to-Date

Keep up-to-date about cyberbullying by frequently researching on the Internet. Entire books have been written on this topic, and I'm sure the content of this chapter has raised many questions. There is still much more to know. I encourage you to visit the web sites listed here to find out more about preventing and stopping cyberbullying.

A Sampling of Web Sites with Information About Cyberbullying and Internet Safety

www.stoptextbully.com

www.cyberbullyinghelp.com

www.cyberbullying.ca

www.cyberbullying.org

www.stopcyberbully.org

www.cyberbullying.us

www.wiredsafety.org

www.ncpc.org/parents/cyberbullying.php

www.isafe.org

www.csriu.org

www.netfamilynews.org

www.safekids.com

www.internetsafe.org

www.cybertipline.com

http://ifc.gospelcom.net

Following are additional web sites you should know about.

PostSecret. This popular site is the online home of an ongoing community art project that encourages users to mail in a secret anonymously on one side of a homemade postcard. New secrets are posted on the site every Sunday, and the site has already yielded a best-selling book. Note, however, that some entries contain graphic images. (www.postsecret.blogspot.com)

Live Journal. This web site allows teens and others to express themselves in an online diary format, or blog. Offers insight into the personal lives of our teens. (www.livejournal.com)

Diary Project. This "global multimedia resource encourages teens to write about their day-to-day experiences growing up." Teens can share their innermost secrets and feelings anonymously, with "honesty, openness, and connectedness." (www.diaryproject.com)

KEY MESSAGES

- Tell your child that it is important that you have open lines of communication with one another.

- Gather information and determine the facts about cyberbullying events.

- Teach your child that the Golden Rule also applies when using technology.

- Explain rules of cyber-safety to your child.

- Frequently monitor your child's use of the computer and provide supervision of its use.

- Make certain web sites off-limits for your child.

- Tell your child not to interact with bullies through a cell phone or through computers.

- Keep copies and a careful record of any bullying activity.

- You may want to report a bullying event to a specific web site, your ISP, or even the police.

8

Neighborhood Bullying

Dear Dr. Beane:

My seven-year-old son is constantly being bullied by a group of ten-year-olds down the street. I've tried talking to their parents, but of course, they refuse to believe their sons are anything less than angels. I've tried talking to the school principal, who says as long as it happens off school grounds, there's nothing he can do. I spoke with the police, who say that because of their age, there's not much they can do except talk to their parents, which of course, puts me back at square one. Short of moving, what can I do to protect my child?

In recent years, much has been written about preventing and stopping bullying in our schools. Several states have mandated that schools have policies and procedures for reporting and responding to it. However, neighborhood bullying hasn't received the attention it deserves. Everyone has the right to feel safe in their neighborhood. Bullying occurs everywhere in the community—in homes, schools, recreation areas, workplaces, churches, neighborhoods, and so on. Bullying is a community issue, and all the resources of the community should be used to prevent and stop it. It must not be tolerated anywhere.

Most quality anti-bullying programs encourage community involvement, but sometimes fail to offer guidance for parents on how to deal with bullies in their neighborhood. Some desperate parents have even contemplated moving to a more peaceful location.

The purpose of this chapter is to give you a few strategies to consider when your child is bullied in the neighborhood. Of course, other strategies presented in this book can also be used, especially the strategies in Chapter 6. Some of the following are unique to neighborhood bullying.

Provide Emotional Support

Your first step is to provide emotional support for your child and give her hope that the bullying will stop. She needs help not only in dealing with the bullies but also in dealing with her feelings and thoughts.

Some victims become convinced they deserve to be bullied. Some even feel they are defective as human beings and expect to be mistreated. Let your child know that no one deserves to be bullied. Explain that bullies seek to hurt and control because they have such problems as lack of self-control or because they may have been mistreated by someone themselves.

Stay calm even though you are concerned about your child's safety. When you get mad and excited, it concerns your child. She will feel that you are not capable of handling her situation appropriately, that you might make it worse.

Be sensitive to the fact that your child may feel embarrassed and ashamed because she can't physically stand up for herself. There is usually a power imbalance. The bullies are stronger, have psychological power over her, and often outnumber her. Let your child know that it is normal to feel hurt, fear, and anger. Help her express these in appropriate ways. Ask your child to write down in a journal or notebook her thoughts and feelings about what has happened. This can be very therapeutic.

Express confidence that you, with the help of others, will find a solution. Don't promise that you will not tell anyone. You may need help. Involve your child in discovering solutions to her bullying situation. Sometimes children have tremendous insight into their own problems.

Involve your child in service projects and projects that involve helping others. Helping others can have a healing effect on victims of bullying. It makes them feel valued and gives them a sense of accomplishment.

Help your child develop a "best friend." Children who have one best friend are bullied less often, are emotionally better able to deal with the bullying, and have fewer behavior problems resulting from the mistreatment.

Help your child develop a skill or hobby that can serve as an emotional and expressive outlet and even net some social prestige for them. Help your child identify her talents and gifts, and if possible, provide the opportunities and the resources needed to develop them. Demonstrating special abilities can help promote the acceptance of your child. People are attracted to, or at least interested in, those who display talents and gifts, especially when they are used skillfully.

Have a Safety Plan

When you first find out that your child is a victim of bullying in the neighborhood, immediately develop a safety plan for her. The first thing you should seek to do is to increase adult supervision of your child. If you cannot be at home to watch your child, ask someone in the family or a trusted friend in the neighborhood to supervise her. If you can't supervise your child after school, enroll her in a quality youth program supervised by adults who you know do a good job of supervising children and youth.

Tell your child never to walk to and from school alone if that is where the bullying happens. Ask siblings or friends who are older and bigger than the bullies to walk with your child if possible.

Ask an older student whom you know and trust to mentor and supervise your child. You could even pay her to supervise your child in the neighborhood when you are unable to do so.

Ask your child to avoid the bullies, if possible. Of course, this is difficult to do in school, but there are places in the neighborhood that are easy to avoid. If your child can avoid certain high-risk places during high-risk times, she should. For example, if your child is being bullied at the video arcade, tell your child to avoid going there.

Ignoring inappropriate behavior can sometimes stop the behavior. However, it may just make the bully work harder to hurt your child by saying meaner and nastier things and by becoming more physical in her attacks. Therefore, if you tell your child to ignore the bully, tell her to try it for only about a week or two and to report its effectiveness to you. Make sure your child understands that you have other suggestions that might be more effective if that doesn't work.

Ask your child to report to you every day regarding how she is being treated. Ask her to keep a journal of the mistreatment. Explain that you will read the journal each day. Examine your child's journal for consistency in what she has told you and what she has written about the bullying events.

Monitor your child's whereabouts and her friendships and ask her to occasionally report in to you by telephone. Ask questions: What did you do today? Who did you sit with today? Who did you play with today? Was everyone nice to you today? Were you nice to others today?

Inform your neighbors about the bullying and ask them to be observant. Form a neighborhood watch program. Encourage neighbors to keep video cameras near their window to record bullying in the neighborhood. Retired individuals might be willing to patrol the neighborhood or sit on their front steps with cameras and scan the area.

Gather and Record Information

Because you may need to report your child's mistreatment to the appropriate authorities, it is important to gather and record information about the bullying events experienced by your child. Keep a log of information. Do not interrogate your child, but conversationally ask questions to determine what has happened, who was involved, when it happened, and where it happened. Look for patterns in this information. Ask yourself what locations and time periods need to be avoided. Also find out if anyone witnessed the bullying. Get their names, addresses, and telephone numbers if possible. This is information you will need to tell law enforcement or court officials.

Take pictures of any injuries and hold a ruler next to the injuries to show their sizes. If your child has been significantly injured, either physically or emotionally, take her to a doctor to have an official record of the physical injuries as well as the emotional trauma. Your doctor can make a referral to specialists that your child may need to see, including a psychologist. Make sure you keep a record of all medical treatment; all medical expenses, including counseling; and all related travel expenses. Also make note if the injuries or the events causing the injuries interrupt your child's sleep pattern.

Because police do not always think to inform parents of all their legal options, you may want to meet with a lawyer to determine the rights of your child and what legal recourse you have. For example, you may be able to file assault charges or get a restraining order. Also ask the lawyer if the parents of the bully can be held responsible for their child's behavior.

Purchase a miniature video camera for your child to videotape any incidents of mistreatment. Cameras are included in most cell phones. Tell her this is the only purpose of the camera and that she will be punished if the device is used inappropriately.

Talk to individuals in the community and find out what you can about the bullies and their families. You do not have to mention that your child is being bullied. This information might give you some insight into the bully's behavior and help you explain to your child why bullies seek to hurt others. You may also discover that the parents of the bully are very good parents and would not be pleased if they knew their child was mistreating others.

Talk to other parents. Perhaps their children are being bullied or have been bullied by the same individual(s). Ask them to keep a log of the mistreatment. Examine the information for consistent patterns (people involved, times, locations, and so on). Determine what they have done to prevent and stop the bullying. Brainstorm ways you can band together to protect your children. Perhaps there is action you can take as a group.

Contact Authorities

If your child is being harassed or physically attacked, file a report with the appropriate juvenile authority. Review the legal information in Chapter Six. Sometimes you don't even have to file a formal written complaint with the police. You can voice your complaint and when the bullied is a juvenile, they will get permission to talk to the bully. Because juvenile law varies from state to state, determine if you can file a formal written complaint (report), to whom you should send the report, and who is to follow the related legal policies and procedures. If you are permitted to file a complaint, include the photographs of your child's injuries, video and/or audio recordings documenting the mistreatment, and your log of information. This information will be important if you go to court, but is sometimes not necessary when you are filing just a complaint, not charges. In some states you will report to a worker designated by the district court assigned to try juvenile cases. This individual often does not seek to determine guilt but rather to find solutions to the conflict. This gives the bullies an opportunity to avoid the court. In some states, if you file a complaint (not charges), the bullies will be asked to engage in an activity (for example, an anger management class, community service). Sometimes the bullies are ordered to stay away from the victim for a significant time period. If they attend school together, the school has to ensure this separation. Usually a contract is signed agreeing to the consequences for their behavior. Unfortunately, the consequences are often not significant enough to stop the bullying. If the contract is broken, more severe consequences are applied. If the bullies deny what has been reported, they have the choice to go to court, rather than sign the contract. Most bullies will not want to go to court. They know they are guilty and that their guilt will be obvious from the evidence. They also run the risk of receiving a more severe punishment (time in a detention center, for example) from the judge. Time in a detention center can vary from two days to a few weeks. If it involves more than thirty days, a less restrictive setting (such as youth boot camp) may be utilized.

Law enforcement officers can be very helpful. Assault and harassment laws apply to people of all ages. Police officers do not have to witness an incident or have evidence of mistreatment before they can talk to a bully. You can ask law enforcement officers to discuss the situation with the bully. If the bully is a juvenile, the officers will seek the parents' permission to speak to her or him. The bully's parents do not have to be present for the questioning, but it is usually good police procedure. They often will read the bully's rights, even when a formal written complaint has not been made. As mentioned in the e-mail at the beginning of this chapter, sometimes parents are told that schools do not have the power or authority to deal with bullying that occurs outside school property. So how can they be of assistance? First of all, the school should take some kind of action, especially if your child is walking to or from school. They are legally responsible for your child walking to and from school.

Most school systems will work with parents and cooperating agencies (such as law enforcement and neighborhood watch groups) to insure the safety of children walking to and from school. For example, the school system can ask the police to patrol particular areas during times children are traveling to and from school. They can also train volunteers to implement a "Walking School Bus" program, which entails adults walking with and supervising students to and from school in the neighborhood.

Even if your child is being bullied other times in the neighborhood, the school can take some kind of action. Inform your child's school about the neighborhood bullying. If the bullies attend your child's school, school personnel need to monitor the bullies' interaction with your child. Ask them to appoint someone in the school to whom your child can report on a daily basis. This could occur weekly to begin with and then change to monthly if the situation improves. Because bullied children sometimes develop behavioral problems themselves, telling school personnel about the bullying may help them understand and deal with your child's behavior if it becomes a matter of concern in future.

Other Tips

• Use your own judgment about contacting the parents of the bullies. Some parents of bullies are terrific parents and will deal with the problem, but sometimes they are not understanding and will not cooperate. See Chapter Six for more on how to interact with the bullies' parents, if you choose to go that route.

- Don't tell your child to retaliate. She may try to equalize the power imbalance with a weapon. She might get hurt or do something to the bully she might regret. Such a recommendation communicates to your child that violence is the way to deal with violence. It also tells her that she is alone in dealing with the situation. She should know that she's not alone—that adults need to be involved in finding the solution.

- Teach your child to be assertive, but not aggressive. See Chapter Six for specific tips on how to respond to bullies. Have your child role-play using these strategies, and pick the ones that seem to work best for your child.

- Involve your child in activities that keep her away from the neighborhood bullies. This will also give her an opportunity to have supportive friends she can talk to.

- Children are hesitant to tell their parents about bullying. When they do, they often have reached the end of their rope and feel helpless; some have even lost hope that things will ever get better for them. Watch for signs of depression in your child and do not hesitate to seek professional counseling for her.

- Help your child build up her body strength, self-confidence, and self-esteem. Teach her to walk upright and to avoid looking like an easy target.

- Monitor your child's behavior toward others. Sometimes victims of bullying start mistreating others. Do not tolerate it. Remind your child to stick to the Golden Rule—treat others the way you want to be treated.

- Ask yourself if there something your child is doing to provoke the bullies. Is it something that your child could stop doing?

- Host a community meeting on bullying prevention. Invite an expert on bullying to address the nature of bullying, its destructiveness, why it must be prevented and stopped in neighborhoods, and what role community members play. Invite parents in the neighborhood, law enforcement officials, school personnel, and representatives of faith-based organizations, and encourage everyone to contribute ideas.

• Consider teaching kids in the neighborhood to band together and protect each other in nonviolent ways. This is called being an empowered bystander. If other children are witnessing the bullying and ignoring it, they are part of the problem. See Chapter Eleven for more tips on how to empower bystanders.

• Ask churches in your community to address bullying and to drive home the importance of obeying the Golden Rule. I am an ordained minister, and I often speak in churches on this topic. I speak to adults and youth. If you're a religious person, pray for your child and pray that the bullies will change. Ask local churches to place the issue of bullying on their prayer lists.

• Because bullies also need help, find community programs that seek to help troubled youth and can reach out to the bullies. By helping the bullies change, you will be helping your child.

• Ask the schools to implement an anti-bullying program and to have an expert on bullying speak to the students, parents, and teachers. Bullying in the neighborhood often starts in the school.

• Share with your child the other strategies mentioned in this book. Also search the Internet for helpful material. Don't give up, and every day, tell your child that you love her and give her lots of hugs. Spend time with her and ask about her day.

KEY MESSAGES

- Bullying is a community issue, and all the resources of the community should be used to prevent and stop it.

- Provide emotional support for your child and give her hope that the bullying will stop.

- Let your child know that no one deserves to be bullied.

- Explain that bullies seek to hurt and to have power and control over others.

- Take pictures of all injuries and hold a ruler next to the injuries to show their sizes; take your child to the doctor to document the injuries and trauma of the experience.

- If your child is being harassed or physically attacked, file a report with the appropriate juvenile authority.

- When you first find out that your child is a victim of bullying, immediately develop a safety plan for her.

- Start a neighborhood watch program.

- Use technology to document the mistreatment.

- Ask the schools to implement an anti-bullying program.

- Ask the schools to recommend that police patrol the areas of concern.

- Ask the schools to implement a Walking School Bus program.

- Host a community meeting on bullying prevention.

- Consider teaching kids in the neighborhood to band together and protect each other in nonviolent ways.

9

Supportive Tips for Siblings

Dear Dr. Beane:

You have done a couple of lectures at schools my children attend. I have spoken with you a few times in regards to bullying issues present in our district which affect my children. I have three sons who are being bullied. My oldest daughter writes poetry and handed me a poem which she had done for one of her English classes. Some of it is fictional.

Too Late

Walking home from school,
I wonder who will be next to meet the cruel.
The teachers and principal don't care,
But when you meet these people, you can't help but stare,
No understanding for a source of such hate,
Who would think that children could harbor such a trait?

I finally arrive at my house,
Silently and slowly I creep inside, just like a mouse.
I hope he did not become the target of a fight.

Panicking like a lost child, I call my mom,
She has no answer about lost Tom.
The police are my next call,
Looks like I'm not going to the mall.

After, all I could do was sit and wait,
For Tom to come home, as I wondered his fate.
As the clock strikes four,
Still no knock on the door.
A breaking of silence, as the phone rings,
Mother is on the line whimpering something.

Once I am able to figure it all out,
I throw down the phone, as I scream and shout.
The words echo in my head,
"Tom was beaten up and now he's dead."
It's not in my nature to hate or kill,
Yet those were my thoughts, which I think of still.

—by a concerned sibling

This poem conveys the significant impact her brother's mistreatment had on this girl as his sibling and communicates the hurt, fear, frustration, and anger that many siblings can experience when they see their brother or sister bullied. They too feel powerless and need to be empowered to support and encourage their brother or sister.

If your child is being bullied, get his permission to share the following information with his siblings. In fact, this is good information to share with all your children before anyone is mistreated.

• Whenever your sibling tells you about his mistreatment, you should feel special. Victims of bullying usually prefer to share this information with their friends, not their siblings. Knowing about the bullying gives you the opportunity to play a valuable helping role in your sibling's life. He will never forget how you helped.

• Don't make fun or make light of the situation. Bullying is serious and can cause physical and emotional health problems. Bullying is destructive to the well-being of individuals and creates unsafe schools.

- Don't promise to keep the bullying a secret. Tell your sibling that you love him and care too much about him not to help. Tell him that you are obligated to tell your parents or a trusted adult, but that you will try to ensure that the situation is handled in an appropriate manner.

- Make sure he realizes that the bullying is not his fault and that he is not expected to deal with the problem alone. It is not just his problem. Adults should get involved. It has been proven over and over that when adults get involved, bullying can be prevented and stopped. Encourage him to tell your parents or a trusted adult. Tell him that you will go with him to support him. If he is willing, he should tell someone at school. He could take a trusted friend with him to tell the adult. He could also ask the adult to keep his name confidential.

- Even if he tells you that he will tell your parents later, keep a log (record) of the bullying events he shares with you. Record what happened, as well as when and where it happened. Also record who was involved (including witnesses). Ask if he has told any adults about it. If so, ask whether the adults took any action to stop it. If so, ask what action was taken. Getting answers to these questions will make it easier for you to share the information with your parents or another trusted adult. Write this information down as soon as you can. Don't overload your sibling emotionally by asking a lot of questions.

- If you go to the same school as your sibling, try to defend him verbally. Be assertive with the bully, but don't threaten him. Tell your friends who are bigger and stronger than the bully so that they can help defend your sibling in a nonviolent but assertive manner. If it seems appropriate, take your friends with you to tell the bully to leave your sibling alone. Don't start a fight, but be assertive. Tell your sibling to let you know if the bully says anything about the confrontation. Tell him that if the bully teases him about having help from you and your friends, he could respond with something like "Isn't it great to have friends like that?" and then walk off confidently.

• Be a good listener. Seek to understand the feelings of your sibling and spend time with your sibling in fun activities after school and on weekends. Don't feel as if you need to respond to every comment. Simply indicate that you understanding the feeling behind the words.

• Maintain open lines of communication with your parents. Keep them posted on the mistreatment of your sibling. Do not exaggerate—just share the facts.

• When you hear rumors about your brother or sister, share them with your sibling and your parents. Keep in mind that the best way to stop rumors is to confront the person spreading the rumor—to let him know that he is being hurtful.

KEY MESSAGES

• The sibling should not make fun or make light of the situation.

• The sibling should not promise to keep the bullying a secret.

• The sibling should encourage his brother or sister to tell an adult, or volunteer himself to tell an adult.

• If bigger and stronger, the sibling could try to assertively defend his brother or sister.

• The sibling could enlist his friends who are bigger and stronger than the bully to help his sibling in a nonviolent but assertive manner.

• The sibling should be a good listener.

• The sibling should maintain open lines of communication with his brother or sister and the parents.

10

When Your Child Bullies Others

Dear Dr. Beane:

On your web site you recommend that parents of victims not contact the parents of the bully, unless they know these parents will take action to correct their children. I found that offensive. It seems to imply that all parents of bullies are bad parents. Our son is five years old and mistreats others. We have tried everything we can think of to change his behavior. Nothing seems to work. Now he is receiving professional counseling. I just wanted you to know not all parents of bullies are bad parents. When you speak to people, would you please share this fact with them?

The parent who sent this e-mail to me is correct; as I've mentioned several times in this book, it is wrong to assume that all parents of bullies are bad parents. When good parents find out that their child is mistreating others, it is shocking, heartbreaking, unbelievable, and troubling. But good parents can have children who go astray, and these parents want to know when their child is bullying others. After all, children who bully are at risk for other forms of antisocial behavior, such as juvenile delinquency, criminality, and substance abuse. In fact, they may even be at risk for health problems. Therefore, if your child is a bully, you should feel a sense of urgency to help your child change.

If your child is a victim, she is at risk of becoming a bully. Therefore, this chapter is relevant for parents of both victims and bullies.

Possible Warning Signs That Your Child May Bully Others

It is critical to be sensitive to signs that your child has adopted beliefs and has attitudes and thoughts that lead to hurtful or destructive behavior, such as bullying. Some of those warning signs appear here. Your child may be a bully if she

- Enjoys feeling powerful and in control
- Seeks to dominate or manipulate others (or both)
- Brags about her actual or imagined superiority over peers
- Is popular with other students who envy her power
- Is impulsive and easily angered, and has low tolerance of frustration
- Loves to win at everything, hates to lose at anything, and is a poor winner (boastful)
- Seems to derive satisfaction or pleasure from others' fear, discomfort, or pain
- Seems overly concerned with others "disrespecting" her; equates respect with fear
- Seems to have little or no empathy or compassion for others
- Seems unable or unwilling to see things from another person's perspective or to "walk in someone else's shoes"
- Seems willing to use and abuse other people to get what she wants
- Defends her negative actions by insisting that others "deserve it," "ask for it," or "provoke it"; a conflict is always someone else's fault

- Is good at hiding negative behaviors or engaging in them where adults can't see her

- Gets excited when conflicts arise between others

- Stays cool during conflicts in which she is directly involved

- Exhibits little or no emotion (flat affect) when talking about her part in a conflict

- Blames other people for her problems

- Refuses to accept responsibility for her negative behaviors

- Shows little or no remorse for her negative behaviors

- Lies in an attempt to stay out of trouble

- Expects to be "misunderstood," "disrespected," and picked on; attacks before she can be attacked

- Interprets ambiguous or innocent acts as purposeful and hostile; uses these as excuses to strike out at others verbally or physically

- "Tests" your authority by committing minor infractions, then waits to see what you'll do about them

- Disregards or breaks school and class rules

- Is generally defiant or oppositional toward adults

- Seeks or craves attention and seems just as satisfied with negative attention as positive attention

- Attracts more than the usual amount of negative attention from others; is disciplined more often than other children

- Seems mainly concerned with her own pleasure and well-being

- Seems antisocial

- Has a close network of friends (actually "henchmen" or "lieutenants") who follow along with whatever she wants to do, even when it is wrong

What You Can Do

First of all, you should review the material in Chapters Three and Four. You may discover parenting gaps that need to be filled and some topics that you need to review with your child.

Next, be careful about labeling your child a bully. I don't think children should be labeled "bullies" any more than they should be labeled "victims." We should just identify the strengths and problems that a child has and address them. If we label children as bullies, they may seek to behave like bullies.

Be thankful you know about the bullying, and take the problem seriously. Don't ignore it, and don't deny that your child could be a bully. You need to avoid feeling defensive. When someone expresses disapproval of your child's behavior, do not see it as an attack on your parenting practices. Good parents can't be perfect, and children aren't perfect. Parenting is one of the most difficult jobs on this earth, and children are complex human beings who are always exploring the limits of behavior, especially when parents aren't around. By honestly facing the facts, you will be increasing the likelihood that your child will be happy. You may or may not have observed the bullying behavior of your child. Bullies try not to behave like bullies in the presence of adults, especially in front of their parents who have tried to apply consequences for inappropriate behavior. This is especially characteristic of girl bullies. The more time you spend discussing bullying with your child, the easier it will become for your child to talk about it. In addition, always compliment your child for her willingness to share information with you, even information that may disappoint you.

If someone tells you that your child was involved in bullying another child, don't get upset or angry. Try to stay calm and guard against showing your anger through your facial expressions and other nonverbal signals, as well as tone of voice. Be willing to believe that your child is mistreating others. All children have the capacity to be bullies. It may be that your child is simply following the lead of others. Your child may be afraid not to participate in the bullying. Ask your child if she is fearful of becoming a victim. It is easier to change a follower's behavior than the behavior of a bully.

Try to find out why your child is mistreating others. Search for the causes. Why is this important? Once you discover the causes, you can apply the corrective strategies provided in this book to reverse the behavior. You will want to involve your child in this journey to discover reasons for her behavior. However, keep in mind that most children who bully will minimize or deny wrongdoing. Don't accept such excuses as "It was all in fun" or "She brings it on herself." There should not be anything fun about belittling or degrading someone. No one deserves to be bullied, not even those who provoke your child or whom your child dislikes. The Golden Rule doesn't say treat others the way you want to be treated only if they don't irritate you or if you like them.

Discovering possible reasons for the bullying requires you to ask your child, and yourself, some questions. Again, Chapters Three and Four will be very helpful in this effort. The following are some questions you might ask yourself about your child:

- What is happening right before my child misbehaves that might be provoking her behavior?

- What happens immediately after my child misbehaves that might be encouraging her to continue the behavior?

- Is my child acting out of anger? Is my child an angry child?

- Does my child misbehave to get attention?

- Is my child's behavior motivated by self-centeredness or jealousy? Does my child lack self-control?

- Is my child testing my limits with her inappropriate behavior?

- Does my child lack empathy and sensitivity toward the feelings of others?

- Is my child watching too much violence in movies and video games?

- Are there any patterns to her behavior (people she's with, times, days, places, and so on)?

Then there are questions you and your spouse (if you are married) need to ask about yourselves, such as the following:

- Is my child imitating me or someone else at home?

- Is my child mistreated at home and therefore taking her anger out on others at school?

- Have we taught our child the Golden Rule?

- Have we helped her develop empathy and sensitivity for the feelings of others?

- Have we helped her develop self-control by consistently setting limits on her behavior?

- Have we consistently applied negative corrective consequences for inappropriate behavior?

- Have we been too critical?

- Have we praised and rewarded her for appropriate behavior?

- Have we taught her how to express her feelings appropriately?

- Have we taught her not to be prejudiced and to respect all people as humans of value?

Remember that bullies mistreat others for a lot of reasons, the most common being (1) to have power and control; (2) to hurt; (3) to express feelings of anger, insecurity, loneliness, and so on; and (4) for the fun of it. Sometimes children mistreat others because parents or siblings mistreat them at home. Sometimes they even bully siblings because they are mistreated at school.

Ask your child if there is anything that is making her upset or angry or sad. Ask her if she feels that these things are making her mistreat others. If your child is young, she may be better able to express herself through drawing or through play. For example, you may notice that when she is "playing school" with her dolls, she seems to use a lot of angry words or creates angry interactions.

When the time seems right, ask your child about the bullying incident to find out what occurred. Avoid using "you" statements. When you start statements with "you," your child may feel that she is being attacked. Be sure to listen to your child's description of what happened, without interrupting. Listen to what your child says about her actions and the actions of the victim(s). Try to find the answers to the following questions, which, not coincidentally, are very similar to the questions you would ask your child if she had experienced bullying herself:

- Who was involved?
- What was said and done by your child and others?
- What happened or usually happens immediately before the bullying occurs?
- Who were the bystanders, and what did they say and do?
- When did or does the bullying occur?
- Where did or does it happen?
- Was there any adult supervision?
- Are there video cameras in the area recording activities?
- What happened or usually happens after the bullying event?
- Who has been told about the bullying, and what have they done (if anything)?
- How long has this been occurring?

Avoid having a knee-jerk reaction to your child's comments. After listening, ask questions to fill in the gaps, but don't interrogate your child. Don't overload your child emotionally by asking too many questions at once. During the process of listening to your child, you may discover why she is mistreating others. If not, wait until you think the time is right to ask her why she thinks the bullying happens. If you ask too soon, your child may not share everything with you or may not tell the truth. It is important to have the facts about what has happened. Sometimes children leave out critical information that affects our understanding of what occurred. Keep in mind that the "Why did you . . . ?" line of questions rarely works with anyone, even adults. If the conversation gets heated, call for a break so that everyone can calm down. It will be easier to discuss it with your child when everyone is calmer.

Find out what other parents and students know about the individuals who claim to be victimized. When you talk to them, don't mention the bullying; just seek information in an informal way. Don't criticize the individuals who say they were victims.

If the parents of bullying victims have given the school a log specifying the dates and times your child has mistreated their children, ask for a copy of the log and check the dates and times. If you continue to receive reports of your child's behavior, keep your own log (record) of the bullying events. This will make it easier for you to check the facts as you gather information and as you hear information repeated.

Ask your child to write down in a journal or notebook her thoughts and feelings about what has happened. Ask your child for permission to read what is written. Help her work through her emotions and thoughts about the bullying. You can then cross-check journal notes with your conversations with your child and with the information shared by others.

Help your child see errors in her thinking. For example, your child may blame everything on the victims and be blind to her own quick temper, lack of self-control, disrespect, and lack of sensitivity. Help your child examine the facts as well as her perceptions of what happened.

Does your child feel embarrassed and ashamed of her behavior? This is not usually the case with true aggressive bullies. However, some good kids find themselves bullying others "because everyone else is." If your child is joining the bullying to be popular, tell her that kindness and integrity are more important than popularity. If your child does regret her actions, praise her feelings and develop a plan of action (including apology and restitution). Explain to your child that you appreciate her feelings, but because you love her, there must also be consequences for the behavior. Ask your child to apologize for her bullying and make restitution—make amends. The apology could be verbal or in writing. Explain that you will check to see if the victim received an apology. Explain that a willingness to apologize is a reflection of good character. Also explain that even if the victim doesn't accept the apology, your child has done the right thing.

Apply negative consequences for bullying, such as withholding privileges, requiring restitution, and so on, that are in proportion to the severity of her behavior, as well as appropriate for her age and stage of development. Coming up with the appropriate consequences can be difficult because for some children even "mild" bullying can be very hurtful. Sometimes just talking to your child is not very effective. Consequences should be administered in a consistent and warm manner, not in the heat of anger. You should also praise your child for appropriate behavior. Praise is very powerful.

Tell your child that a person's reputation is more valuable than gold. It is important that she have a good name. Tell her that people will remember all their lives how she treated them. Discuss how mistreatment is often remembered for a lifetime, and discuss the disadvantages of creating memories like that in the minds of others. Stress how it could impact her future. Also discuss how kindness is often remembered for a lifetime. Discuss the advantages of creating memories like that in others. Ask her to describe her current reputation as it relates to how she treats others. Ask her, "When people hear your name, what do they remember, and what do they think about?"

If your child has been bullying others at school, tell her that you will support the school as it applies punishment and that you will not make excuses for her behavior. The school may consider suspending or expelling her from school. If you have a copy of the school's anti-bullying policy, read it to your child and explain it to her. Make sure she understands the consequences. Also explain that you may apply additional consequences.

Depending on the age of your child and the nature of the bullying behavior, tell her that she could get into legal trouble for mistreating others. If the mistreatment is very serious, some parents of bullying victims file assault charges or get a restraining order against the bully.

Ask your child if she has any ideas about what needs to happen for the bullying to stop. Children are sometimes very perceptive and have a lot of insight into their relational problems. Write down her suggestions and review them by examining the pros and cons of each.

Remind your child that it is often those who are feeling small, afraid, weak, and helpless that resort to violence by retaliating. Explain that hurt students have hurt others. When they retaliate, they go after those who have mistreated them, and they often hurt innocent bystanders.

Communicate zero tolerance of bullying. Set limits and immediately stop any aggression. Your child will probably appreciate limits, even though she would never tell you. Limits will give her a sense of security because they add structure to her life—creating a feeling that things are controllable. When there are no limits, life can seem to be out of control, and your child may feel that anything could happen to her. Your child may mistreat others to have control over her relationships.

Teach your child to control her anger. Teach her to get away from situations that anger her. Review with your child the anger management techniques listed in Chapter Four. Help your child find nonaggressive ways to express her feelings. Tell your child to use the anger management strategies discussed in Chapter Four. In addition, teach your child to rehearse in her mind the self-talk statements listed here:

Positive Self-Talk

- I can make positive memories that could last a lifetime in people's minds.
- I can control my anger.
- I can have power and control by doing good things, such as helping others.
- I do not have to mistreat others just because I feel I am being mistreated.
- I will have more true friends if I am kind to others and control my anger.
- I will not hurt others when I am angry.
- I have a good heart and I can do what my good heart tells me to do.
- I can be kind to others.
- Today is going to be a good day and I'm going to treat others right.
- People are nice and are going to be nice to me today.
- Most people will treat me with respect when I treat them with respect.
- When I am angry, I will talk to an adult about it.
- When I am frustrated and have bad thoughts, I will talk to an adult about them.

Make sure your child gets a good night's sleep. Lack of sleep affects self-control and the ability to make good decisions and therefore may affect how your child chooses to treat others. It also affects mood and feelings, which can affect behavior.

Make sure your child exercises regularly and eats the right foods. One of the greatest things your child can do is to stay healthy. This will help her deal with stress in a healthy way instead of by lashing out at others.

Be an observant parent. Because bullying can occur over cell phones and over the Internet, monitoring your child's behavior will sometimes be difficult. Therefore, when you can't observe your child's behavior, ask questions and examine her cell phone and computer for inappropriate material and patterns of possible inappropriate behavior.

Give your child something meaningful to do at home. Assign chores to your child and communicate your expectations of how and when the chores should be done. This will help your child develop a sense of responsibility and feel valued. Express your appreciation for her being helpful and dependable. This will help reinforce positive behavior in your child.

Meet with other parents of bullies and seek to help each other help your children. You can benefit from these relationships. You may hear about strategies that can be used at school and in your homes that are effective for your child, and you may discover who at your child's school is most supportive of preventing bullying.

Your child may benefit from counseling. Because the school counselor often doesn't have the time to give your child the attention she needs, you may decide to secure a professional counselor. If you are a member of a religious organization, you may also want to seek pastoral counseling for her.

If you decide to send your child to a professional counselor, try to prepare her for the first meeting. You do this by reviewing the following questions with her: What has happened? How often do you mistreat others? How long have you been mistreating others? When and where do you do this? Who is involved? What do the bystanders do? How do you feel about what is happening? Does it make you feel good or bad? What do you think should be done? Who are the adults you feel could help you?

Talk to the victim's parents and apologize for your child's behavior. You could even take your child with you and ask her to apologize to the parents and the victim. Explain that you plan to do all you can to make sure the bullying doesn't happen again. Ask them if there is any information they wish to share with you. If the timing seems appropriate, share what information you have gained and then compare notes. Be prepared to hear some things you don't want to hear or find difficult to believe about your child. Just thank the parents for sharing with you. Don't stay too long. If the parents are very angry, state your apology again and tell them you'll come back at a better time.

Promote anti-bullying activities through local PTAs (or PTOs). Ask that bullying be placed on the agenda of a meeting and that a guest speaker be invited to address the topic. Ask local parent organizations, civic organizations, or corporations to sponsor an anti-bullying workshop or to purchase anti-bullying brochures, posters, and books for the school system or school.

When it is known that your child is trying to improve her behavior, children who bully others may attempt to provoke her to join in the mistreatment of others. Warn your child of this behavior. Teach her to remove herself quickly from such situations. Teach her to be assertive and to refuse to let them control her heart and behavior.

Monitor the whereabouts of your child and increase your supervision of her activities. If necessary, go to school with your child one day or more. Sometimes this is enough to make her behave. Let your child know that you believe she can treat others appropriately and that when you see evidence of change, you will back off on your supervision; remind her, however, that you will be ready to step it up again at any moment she resumes mistreating others.

If your child feels bad about herself, seek to improve her self-esteem. Frequently remind her of her positive characteristics and successes. Provide opportunities for success and for experiences that help her feel valued and appreciated. Most of all, remind her of your unconditional love for her. Your love for her will help her love herself and accept herself. Self-acceptance is the basis for self-improvement, and self-love is the basis for compassion toward others.

Help your child develop interests and learn a new hobby or develop a new skill, such as painting, drawing, or playing an instrument. This might help your child feel good about herself. Further, interests that involve structured and well-supervised group activities can encourage cooperative behavior in your child.

Examine your child's friendships and provide opportunities for her to select individuals to be with who seem to have a good reputation. Develop a moral, religious, and spiritual network around your child. Psychologists and other mental health professionals have found that supportive religion can make a big difference in the lives of children, especially adolescents.

Help your child discover that there is power and control in doing good deeds. Involve your child in charitable and community service activities. Find opportunities for your child to help others. When you are asked to help someone, ask your child to accompany you if that is appropriate. When your child does assist you, compliment her personally and publicly when she is present. Let her see that she has pleased you by helping others. Afterwards, discuss with her the pleasure and insights gained by being involved in helping activities.

Ask her to monitor her behavior and report back to you. You may even ask her to keep a journal or notebook of her positive and negative interactions with others. Ask her to record her response to the negative interactions. Tell her you will be reviewing the journal with her to discuss the content.

When you see your child exhibiting sensitivity, kindness, and empathy, reward her with a special treat or privilege. Rewarding positive behavior is very powerful. Sometimes children learn more by being rewarded for appropriate behavior than they do by being punished for inappropriate behavior.

Role-play situations where your child might respond inappropriately. For example, what should she do when someone accidentally knocks her books off her desk or bumps her in the hallway? This will give your child practice in controlling her anger. Role playing also teaches appropriate behavior.

Make sure your discipline style is not too permissive or too aggressive. Your discipline must be firm, controlled, and full of love. Good discipline helps your child develop the self-control necessary for her to stop bullying.

Examine your own behavior. Are you modeling overly aggressive behavior? Are you bullying your child? Do you frequently criticize your child? Do you use your words to build people up, to encourage and support others, or do you cut people down with your words?

Ask an older child or young adult who has good morals to mentor your child. Mentoring can be effective. The mentor can go places with your child and do a lot of fun things with her. She can also provide guidance on what is right and wrong and show your child how to have power and control by doing good.

Make sure you have set realistic behavioral change goals for your child and given her time to change. Her inappropriate behavior did not develop overnight. She will therefore need time to learn to manage her feelings, thoughts, and actions. Continually encourage her as she strives to do so.

You can do a lot to help your child stop bullying others, but she must also seek to change herself. Show her the following tips for ways to stop herself from bullying. Not all tips are appropriate for all children. Select some of the tips that you feel are appropriate and teach them to your child.

Tips for Stopping Bullying Behavior

- Frequently remind yourself of the Golden Rule—treat others the way you want to be treated.

- Ask yourself, "Why am I mistreating others?"

- Are you unhappy about something or angry about something that you need to discuss with an adult? If you are, talk to someone about it instead of taking it out on another person.

- Ask yourself, "Do I mistreat others because I am mistreated elsewhere and don't want to be mistreated everywhere?"

- Realize that if you keep on mistreating others you could get into a lot of trouble. You could be suspended or expelled from school or get into trouble with the law.

- Keep in mind that those who are feeling small, afraid, weak, and helpless are often the first to resort to violence and retaliation. When they retaliate, they go after those who have mistreated them and may end up hurting anyone they see, even those who have been kind to them. In this way, you may accidentally cause them to hurt others.

- Sometimes mistreating someone becomes a habit. But you can stop. You can change. Bullying is a choice. Talk to someone about your need to change.

- Perhaps you have fallen into the trap of mistreating someone because "everyone" is doing it. If this is the case, you may feel guilty and need to ask someone to help you get out of the trap. Share your thoughts and feelings with an adult. If you wish, take a friend with you. If you cannot tell the adult personally, then write a note to her explaining what has happened. If you cannot tell your parents, then tell your grandparents, uncle, or aunt—any adult you trust. If you cannot tell your teacher, then tell some other adult in the school. Tell her what is happening, who is involved, who the bystanders are, and where and when it is happening.

- Make sure you get a good night's sleep, exercise regularly, and eat the right foods. All of these will help you have better self-control.

- Don't get defensive if your parents or other adults increase their supervision of your activities. Be thankful that they care enough about you to help you behave more appropriately. Everyone needs somebody who holds her accountable for her actions.

- Listen to the suggestions of your parents and teachers.

Talking to the School

If the bullying happened at school, your next step is to talk to school personnel and let them know that you are aware of your child's behavior and that she is willing to improve (if this is the truth). Make an appointment with your child's teacher and make a factual report, using your log. Most of the time, it is difficult to reach a teacher immediately, but you can get a number or an e-mail address from the school web site or office and leave a message. When you make contact, briefly explain why you wish to meet with her and suggest a time after school, if possible. If you wish, you could briefly describe what is happening. You want to be able to collaborate with the teacher, so try to create a working relationship with her. Give her time to prepare for the meeting.

At the meeting, review your child's situation. Discuss who is involved; what has happened; the dates, times, and locations of the events; who *seems* to be the victim or victims; who are witnesses; and so on. Explain your understanding that some of the information may need to be confirmed and the accuracy checked. If you believe that your child has been doing the bullying, express that you are concerned about your child's behavior and that you need the school's assistance to help her change her behavior. Ask the teacher for suggestions and ideas. Be sure to give her time to talk. At this point, she may not be able to explain what is happening, but at least you have made her aware of the problem. If you wish, schedule a follow-up meeting for the purpose of developing a plan of action. When the meeting is over, thank her for taking time to meet with you.

After the meeting, send a letter to the teacher thanking her again for meeting with you. The letter should also list the agreed-on actions to be taken and the date and time of the follow-up meeting to develop a plan of action. If you wish, send a copy of the letter to the principal. However, make sure you are complimentary of the teacher's professionalism, sensitivity, and concern, if this seems appropriate.

If it appears that the teacher is unable to help your child, even after two or three revisions of the plan of action, schedule a meeting with the principal. Explain that the teacher has been professional and cooperative, but needs some assistance. Ask the principal to make a commitment to take action and ask her to recommend the next steps. If you agree on any the steps, ask for a time frame in which they will be implemented. Then schedule a follow-up meeting with the principal to discuss the effectiveness of the implementation and what should be done next.

Ask for the appropriate school personnel to assist you in applying consequences for inappropriate behavior and to reward appropriate behavior seen in your child. Don't give up. Most school personnel will respond favorably to your concerns. However, if someone ignores you, don't let her brush you off. Don't let anyone minimize your child's behavior or make you feel as though you are taking up too much of her time. You child's safety and health must be a priority—some victims retaliate. By stopping bullying, you are helping your child, other children, and the school.

As strategies are implemented, schedule follow-up appointments with the appropriate school personnel to assess whether action taken by the school has been successful. Try to be patient, but expect action to be taken by the school in a timely manner. Seriously consider any suggestions school personnel give you. Expectations at home need to be consistent with expectations at school.

Ask that there be an adult (that is, a support teacher) to whom your child can talk every day to give an update on her behavior. If the teacher is not responsive, speak to the principal. You must bring this unhealthy situation for your child and other children to an end. Be persistent. Ask the principal to implement an anti-bullying program and provide anti-bullying training for the teachers, bus drivers, counselors, and other adults in the school. School personnel also need to learn how to prevent and stop bullying, how to help victims, and how to change bullies. Ask them to visit the web site www.bullyfree.com. All school personnel need to know how to create schools where all students feel accepted and have a sense of belonging.

KEY MESSAGES

- Even good parents have children who go astray.

- Don't rush to label your child a bully.

- Remind your child of the Golden Rule—treat others the way you want to be treated.

- Stay calm. Don't get angry or defensive when you find out that your child may be bullying others.

- Try to discover why your child is mistreating others.

- Apply negative, yet nonviolent, consequences for bullying.

- Reward positive behavior.

- Support the school's effort to apply consequences for the inappropriate behavior.

- Monitor your child's whereabouts.

- Help your child develop interests and hobbies.

- If necessary, seek professional counseling for your child.

- Examine the appropriateness of your own behavior.

- Examine your discipline style: is it too permissive, too aggressive?

- Give your child tips on stopping bullying behavior.

- Collaborate with the school to help your child.

- Ask the school to implement an anti-bullying program.

11

When Your Child Is a Bystander

Dear Dr. Beane:

After my son heard you speak at his school, one evening he told me a story about a kid in his class. His friends had been bullying and teasing this kid and my son felt guilty that his friends had shunned him from their group. He began to talk with the boy and became his friend. They are now close friends. My son told his group of friends that he was a cool guy if only given the chance. My son told his friends that they weren't his true friends if they didn't accept his friends as well. They are all friends now. I am so glad that my kids share stories like these with me quite often.

If your child is not a victim, a bully, or a follower, he is a bystander. As a bystander, your child has a choice to be part of the solution or part of the problem of bullying. When bystanders choose not to get involved, they join the silent majority that allows bullying to occur. Sometimes bystanders avoid getting involved because they are afraid of the bullies and their followers; at other times it's because they just don't know what to do. They may even be afraid to report the bullying, fearing retaliation or making the situation worse for the victim, or they may just suspect that adults will do nothing anyway.

It is important for your child to know that bullies interpret his noninvolvement as approval and perhaps encouragement to mistreat others. Therefore, it is important for your child to take a stand against bullying and to recruit as many supporters as he can. At first, the number of supporters will be small, but it will grow. The majority of students do not approve of bullying and hope that it will stop. Students can come to realize that there is power in numbers and that they don't have to let a few students control how they treat others. It is important for your child, and other children, to know that they have not only the power but also a responsibility to protect one another in acceptable but effective ways.

We are learning more and more about the different types of bystanders. I believe there are five types, though some experts on bullying count three categories of bystanders: victim bystanders, avoidant bystanders, and ambivalent bystanders.[1]

1. Victim bystanders may identify with the victim and are afraid that they may become a victim if they don't support the bullying. This is a realistic fear, because victim bystanders could very easily become the next targets. They often freeze in fear and do nothing. Sometimes they join the mistreatment and become followers.

2. Avoidant bystanders watch the bullying and don't do anything about it. They may do nothing because they feel there is nothing they can do or because they don't know specifically what to do.

3. Ambivalent bystanders have confused feelings about the bully and the bullying. They are always trying to figure out what role they play in the power dynamics.

I believe we need to consider the following two additional types of bystanders:

4. Empowered bystanders will intervene and seek to support or help the victim. Some students can do this because they have the confidence and power; others have been taught how to support and defend victims.

5. Bully bystanders (followers) willingly encourage the bullying to continue and may even participate in the behavior. They are not usually the ones to initiate the bullying, but they are quick to join in the mistreatment. They may be different from the victim bystander because they have not been victims.

If your child is not a victim but a bystander, you should still be concerned. Researchers have discovered that bystanders who witness bullying sometimes experience increased levels of fear, anxiety, depression, and hopelessness. Even bystanders are hurt when they feel that there is nothing that can be done to stop the bullying.

Ask your child to talk to you about his feelings and thoughts regarding the bullying he sees in school and in the community. Watching bullying around him almost every day can intensify any emotional problems and issues he may already have. Help your child deal with feelings of fear, insecurity, and guilt created by his experience as a bystander. When you first talk to your child about witnessing the bullying, don't overload him emotionally by asking a lot of questions.

Just as it is important for victims of bullying to develop effective coping strategies, it is also important for bystanders to develop certain skills. Bystanders have to be willing to buck the peer system. Help your child understand the importance of not letting someone else control how he treats others. Tell your child that you want him not only to believe the Golden Rule but also to make it a conviction. This means he will let his belief in the Golden Rule control his attitudes, thoughts, and behavior. Express your confidence in your child's ability to do what his good heart tells him to do and not to let anyone else control his heart. Tell your child it is okay to be different by not mistreating someone. You may want to tell your child about some famous people who refused to be molded or shaped by the thinking of others, such as Mother Teresa, Nelson Mandela, Mahatma Gandhi, and Marie Curie.

At some time, every child is a bystander. So share with your child the following tips for dealing with bullying situations he witnesses.

Tips for Bystanders

• Talk to an adult about your feelings and thoughts regarding the bullying you see in school and in the community. Do you feel fearful and unsafe? Do you feel guilty?

• Keep in mind that you and your friends (the other bystanders) outnumber the bullies. You can make a difference.

• Raise the issue of bullying with your friends and at student council meetings, and get permission to raise the issue at faculty and staff meetings. Raise the issue of bullying in your classes (such as social studies, literature, drama, and English). When asked to write an essay or theme in any of your classes, seek to tie the issue of bullying to the topic or, if appropriate, write about bullying.

• When you see someone being mistreated, make a record of the event and tell a trusted adult. Write down what happened, who was involved, and when and where it happened. Also write down what happened immediately before the event and what happened when it was over.

• Ask your friends to join you in making a commitment to help your school be bully free.

• Ask your friends to help you communicate to the bully that bullying will not be tolerated. However, do not mistreat the bully. Take some friends with you to tell the bully to stop mistreating the students you know are victims. Suggest that he speak to someone at school about his anger. Take a stand against the bully. The longer you wait to do this, the more likely you are to join in on the bullying.

• Don't stand watch for the bully and don't watch the mistreatment. The bully wants an audience. You can also try to stop the bullying by going over and standing beside the victim. Ask some friends to join you. Then ask the victim to walk off with you and your friends.

• Take on the characteristic of the victim that the bully is using to mistreat him. For example, you could go over and stand beside the victim and say, "I'm pretty stupid myself; in fact, everybody is stupid in something."

• Refuse to laugh when someone is made fun of or mistreated in some other way; seek to be a peacemaker.

• When you hear gossip, end it by telling the person that you are not going to share the story with anyone and that you feel the person should be told that rumors are being spread about him. Let the victim know that a rumor is being spread about him and that you are trying to stop it.

• Learn to use the assertiveness skills presented in this book. Select those that are appropriate for bystanders. Practice these skills in front of a mirror. They will help you defend victims of bullying. These are not aggressive strategies that hurt the bully; they are ways you can stand up for the victim without provoking the bully. Do not bully the bully, and do not try to deal with the bully on your own.

• Encourage the victim to share his thoughts and feelings with you and, if he can, with an adult. Be a good listener. Ask if he would like for you to report the bullying to an adult.

• Invite the victim to do something with you and your friends, such as going to the movies. Make sure the experience is a positive one.

• Don't let the bullies control how you treat others. Maintain your values and beliefs. Do what is right. Remember, a person's reputation is more valuable than gold. It is important that you have a good name. People will remember all their lives how you treated them. How would you describe your current reputation as it relates to how you treat others? When people hear your name, what do they remember, and what do they think about?

KEY MESSAGES

- Bullies interpret the noninvolvement of bystanders as approval of the bullying.

- Ask your child, the bystander, to discuss his thoughts and feelings regarding the bullying at school.

- Explain to your child the importance of letting his belief in the Golden Rule control his attitudes, thoughts, and behavior.

- Encourage your child to get his friends to campaign against bullying.

- Tell your child not to ignore bullying, not to stand by and watch, and not to laugh at it.

- Encourage your child to learn assertiveness skills so that he can verbally defend victims of bullying.

- Share the tips for bystanders with your child.

12

Why Some Victims Retaliate, Self-Harm, or Commit Suicide

Dear Dr. Beane:

When I was fifteen years old I lost my hair to a skin condition called alopecia. My hair started to fall out. I lost all of my hair on my entire body. When I went to school, teachers and students would make fun of me. I lost my girlfriend also after my hair started to fall out. I recall sitting alone in my Science class because nobody wanted to be by me. One girl told the teacher, "Yuck, I don't want to be by him." The teacher said, "That's okay, you don't have to sit by him." Being an outcast and kids calling me names (egg, Mr. Clean, etc.) started to bother me. When a couple of teachers laughed or smiled when they made fun of me, it destroyed my confidence. I started to skip school by getting off the bus and running into the woods. I came across a group of so-called outcasts. They were kids just like me that weren't accepted by the majority of the school. One day I didn't make it to the afternoon class at school. I drank almost an entire bottle of Southern Comfort and passed out in the woods. The principal discovered me and called an ambulance. I started to drink three to four shots of vodka orange juice in the morning, and smoked a couple of pot

bowls. I hung around other kids that would get in

trouble and take drugs.

This chapter examines the path that some victims of bullying take from hurt to retaliation, self-mutilation, and/or suicide. The information will help you determine if your child is traveling this path and help you prevent her from harming herself or others. This chapter explains the cognitive and psychological processes in which victimized children engage. It is based on my experience with my own son and with other victims who have retaliated and those who have attempted suicide.

It is difficult for some people to have empathy for victims who have retaliated. That's understandable. However, we must ask ourselves what made the victims retaliate. Why do some children go from feelings of deep hurt, fear, overwhelming anxiety, frustration, and helplessness, to experiencing anger, depression, hate, rage, hopelessness, and a desire for revenge or suicide?

The path from hurt to self-mutilation, retaliation, and/or suicide has many elements. You need to understand this path, and so do school personnel. Not all victims who retaliate or harm themselves follow the path perfectly or as sequentially presented in this chapter. The coping stages that victims may pass through in dealing with the trauma of bullying are very fluid, and the elements are often interwoven throughout the stages.[1]

Some victimized children pass through some of the coping stages and never reach the point where they seek to satisfy their desire for revenge and/or suicide—even though the desire is there. One young adult male shared that he often thought about taking a gun to school when he was bullied in high school. He said it was his love for his grandparents that prevented him from satisfying his desire for revenge and later his desire to commit suicide.

Some of the coping stages are more intense for some children than others because of their past life experiences, as well as their biological predispositions, personality, resiliency, and social environment. The age of onset of the victimization, the intensity of the victimization, and the external support available to them are also significant factors.

This chapter may frighten you and cause you a great deal of concern, but you need to be able to determine how well your child is coping with the bullying she is experiencing. There is one truth that should encourage you: victims of bullying are often very resilient individuals. They are often viewed as weak and contributing to their own mistreatment. Such views are unfair. Victims are unbelievably strong, and no one deserves to be bullied. I am often amazed at the incredibly long time that victims put up with persistent mistreatment from peers. Even though the mistreatment flows like a powerful river current, they stay afloat for a long time. I have developed a tremendous admiration for young bullied children. I wish I had their strength of character. It is the bully and the students who join in on the bullying who are weak in character.

Victimization (Persistent Attacks)

The path begins with your child being hurt by bullies, by their followers, and by those who do not defend her, or perhaps even laugh at her. On the surface, the mistreatment may appear to be mild; however, your child may consider it very hurtful and even physically painful.

Accompanying the pain is embarrassment. For example, your child may be teased for some physical trait, so she feels defective and embarrassed. Because your child is overpowered and outnumbered by the bullies, followers, and nonsupportive bystanders, she may also be embarrassed because she can't defend herself as you have taught her to do. She feels like a wimp. These feelings may prevent her from telling you about the mistreatment. As one student said, "Nobody could help me because nobody knew. I was so utterly ashamed of believing I was some kind of wimp I was just too embarrassed to talk about it."[2]

Sometimes the embarrassment leads to humiliation and to intimidation. Not only is the nature of the mistreatment sometimes humiliating, but so is the sense of helplessness. I served as an expert consultant in a criminal case where a high school victim of bullying, I'll refer to him as James, was facing five to ten years in prison for retaliating. He told me several stories about how he was embarrassed and humiliated. He said, "I was so embarrassed. They made me feel like a kindergartener." As initiation onto the basketball team, the freshmen boys had to drink mouthwash. When James drank his bottle of liquid, he discovered that the bully had put urine in his bottle. All year long, students called him "pee drinker." They also put pubic hair on James's pizza. After he ate the pizza, they made fun of him.

This stage can best be described as a mixture of hurt and pain, embarrassment, humiliation, and intimidation. However, at this point the child still has hope that the bullying will end soon.

Anticipatory Anxiety

Because bullying is repeated and persistent mistreatment, it doesn't take long for the child to experience anticipatory anxiety—fear of future victimization. She worries about the same events being repeated. But she also worries about worse things happening. She may worry that the mistreatment will become more physical or that if other family members get involved, they may be harmed.

Anticipating mistreatment causes an almost overwhelming anxiety that can dominate your child's thinking from time to time, especially before the high-risk times (such as when waiting for the bus, riding the bus, and waiting in the common area before school) and before she is required to visit the high-risk areas (bathrooms, stairwells, cafeteria, buses, locker rooms, and so on). Therefore, each day is like a new social minefield.[3] Your child may be overwhelmed with concern about what might be in her path the next day that will hurt her.

This intense anxiety leads to hyperalertness. Your child may have difficulty concentrating and exhibit cognitive disorganization (confused thinking).[4] This has a significant impact on her concentration on academics and her learning. It also affects her ability to make good decisions, including decisions about how to cope with the mistreatment.

This stage adds fear, anxiety, hyperalertness, lack of concentration, confused thinking, and poor decision making to the feelings experienced in the victimization stage. However, the child still has hope that the bullying will end soon.

Revisiting

It is not uncommon for victims of bullying to have recurrent thoughts focused on the bullying and on the associated feelings. Most revisiting seems to occur when the child is alone and is not distracted by other things. For example, lying in bed at night lends itself to revisiting all the times one has been bullied. The child's mind is full of traumatic memories that are almost as real as the events themselves. Victims tell me that they often relive the hurt, embarrassment, humiliation, and fear of each event as if it were actually happening over and over again. The memories can be so real that they are like flashbacks. As a result, some victims have trouble falling asleep and sometimes cry themselves to sleep. When they do fall asleep, nightmares make it difficult to stay asleep. This causes fatigue, which further impacts the child's ability to concentrate, learn, and make good decisions. It may also lead to irritability, impatience, lack of motivation, and feelings of inadequacy. The fatigue may also lead to inappropriate behavior, such as acting disrespectful or uncooperative. The inappropriate behavior is a cry for help.

At this stage of the coping path, your child may experience fatigue, irritability, impatience, lack of motivation, feelings of inadequacy, and inappropriate behavior in addition to the feelings experienced in the earlier stages. However, there is still a ray of hope that the bullying will end soon.

Assessment, Entrapment, Disappointment, Cognitive Disorganization, and Trust Crisis

At some point, your child may assess the seriousness and potential duration of the bullying. When the assessment yields a negative report in your child's mind, she begins to feel overwhelmed, powerless, helpless, and even more inadequate. She may feel trapped in a situation that does not seem to have any possibility of improving. In fact, there is an expectation that the bullying will only get worse, so fear and anxiety increase.

Your child may have observed other children being bullied, with no action taken by adults even after they have been told. Or she may have observed situations getting worse after adults were made aware of the bullying. Victims of bullying have expressed disappointment in the behavior of adults around them. They have seen adults

- Bullying students
- Failing to support other victims—ignoring the victimization
- Lacking empathy
- Giving off reinforcing nonverbal cues that encourage the mistreatment of others
- Laughing at bullying behavior they observe

Unfortunately, some adults have elitist attitudes that communicate, "There are 'us' and there are 'them,' and 'them' just have a difficult time in life. Don't worry about them. Take care of yourself." Such an attitude often leads to ignoring mistreatment or blaming victims for their mistreatment. This is often seen in the labels that adults assign to victims—"loners," "isolated," and "weak."

Sometimes children are bullied by adults. As one student said, "I was bullied by a teacher who was on my back the whole time picking on my work and using me in front of the class as a verbal punching bag."[5] When adults in authority are doing the bullying or when they fail to respond to reports about bullying, the victim's feelings of entrapment increase. They cannot solve the problem on their own, and they also feel that they can't ask another adult to help them.

At this stage, your child's feelings of intimidation and inadequacy are intensified, and her ability to cope with the mistreatment is diminished. This leads to increased stress, feelings of entrapment, and fear. These can hinder your child's ability to concentrate and have a negative impact on learning. Her grades will likely start to drop. In addition, there may be evidence of more cognitive disorganization (confused thinking and poor decision making). It is difficult for any child to learn in an environment where she fears chronic bullying, terrorizing, or intimidation. It is not surprising that the victimized child may have a lower level of motivation and interest in academic activities and be less responsive in class.[6]

This stage also includes feelings of loneliness, abandonment, rejection, and alienation. These intensify the fear that is already present. How intense is this fear? As one student who'd reached this point said, "I've started thinking about suicide. I feel too scared to have a social life. I spend my days in fear both in and out of school."[7]

Your child may find herself in a trust crisis.[8] She begins to lack trust in her ability to cope with or stop the bullying. She may not trust the adults around her to help her. At this point, she may be drowning in self-doubt. She may feel that her only recourse is to take some kind of powerful, drastic action. Such thoughts are initial efforts to gain control over what appears to be an out-of-control social environment. She may or may not be entertaining initial thoughts of self-harm (use of alcohol, drugs, self-mutilation) or retaliation. Such inappropriate thoughts are also permeated with fear that she may succeed at such attempts. Therefore, your child may even hope that someone will rescue her from the temptation to carry out her thoughts. When I let students know that I am aware that they self-mutilate because of bullying, they seem to be eager to tell me they are engaging in such behaviors as "cutting." I have even had students tell me that they are thinking about shooting the bullies or that they have had such thoughts. They seem to want someone to rescue them. One high school student took a gun to school to shoot students who bullied him. When the school resource officer found his gun in his locker, the boy said, "Thank God the police found the gun in my locker. I'm not sure what I might have done."

Such a void of trust may cause your child to wonder if she can trust life to be fair or kind, especially school life. This lack of trust leads to a pessimistic view of life and a proneness to rejection—expecting to be mistreated by peers—which causes intense anxiety about each day. The child wants to be happy at school, but it doesn't seem like a possibility. One student said, "I would rather be at school and be happy like other kids my age but I can't fake it. I don't trust anyone."⁹

If your child has reached this stage of the coping path, she may have experienced a mixture of hurt and pain, embarrassment, humiliation, intimidation, fear, anxiety, hyperalertness, lack of concentration, confused thinking and poor decision making, fatigue, irritability, impatience, lack of motivation, feelings of inadequacy, inappropriate behavior, initial thoughts of retaliation, entrapment, disappointment, lack of trust in people and life, and rejection proneness (expectation of being rejected). However, there is still a ray of hope that the bullying will end soon.

Secrecy, Denial, Avoidance, and Detachment

Secrecy. Victims of bullying find themselves in what can seem like an impossible predicament: to tell an adult or not to tell an adult. Many times, the child's distress is such that she seeks to hide and deny what is happening to her. Unfortunately, bullying thrives on secrecy. So your child may seek to conceal her distress and try to appear okay around you. Sometimes the secrecy is driven by fear that the adults will make the situation worse or that bullies may even seek to harm members of the family.

Denial and conscious inhibition. Embedded in the secrecy is denial and inhibition. This may be a way for your child to protect herself psychologically from feelings associated with her fading hope. She may try to flee her sense of hopelessness by cutting off or disowning thoughts and feelings that threaten and overwhelm her. When this occurs, a narrowing of consciousness occurs, and denial and conscious inhibition become evident. These may be seen when your child recalls only parts of the bullying experience (emotions, feelings, thoughts) and not recall all the details. In fact, she may seek to have no conscious awareness of the bullying and seek distractions to avoid thinking about it, inhibiting thoughts and feelings. The child may even deny and repress her fear. Fear is one of the most difficult feelings to express and a commonly denied feeling. Repressed or denied fear makes life a state of "fear-full-ness." Each day is full of fear. Repressed fear can create worries, anxieties, hypervigilance, phobias, obsessions (including death obsessions), and terror that confuse the child more.

Avoidance and detachment. To accommodate her denial and repressed feelings, your child may seek to avoid everything associated with the bullying, everything that reminds her of the mistreatment and the places where she is at risk of bullying. It's natural to want to withdraw from social experiences that appear risky. This is referred to as avoidance. Avoidance is the most common tactic utilized by victims of bullying.[10] This is especially true when a supervising adult was told about the bullying and did nothing to stop it. Therefore, truancy is common among victims of bullying. In fact, bullying is a precursor of school avoidance.[11] According to the American Medical Association, approximately 160,000 children stay home from school each day because of fear of being mistreated or harmed. Approximately 7 percent of eighth graders skip school at least once a month for fear of being bullied.[12] This inclination is understandable. When adults have suffered mistreatment in specific locations, they tend to avoid those places. They experience the same fear and anxiety. But children do not have the option of avoiding school; by law they must either attend school or be home-schooled. When they feel they are required to go to school, they can feel trapped. This feeling can create even more problems for the child. Several parents have told me that their children were bullied so badly they developed school phobia and had to receive counseling.

When a child's home environment and school environment are abusive, she may run away. Being rejected by loved ones and peers in the two places where you spend most of your time is devastating. A child may thus decide to live on the streets. One student said, "I would rather have a pimp love me than no one at all."

With the child suffering from poor concentration, confused thinking, all of the toxic emotions we have discussed thus far, and school avoidance, it is no wonder that her academic work begins to suffer. Researchers report a significant decrease in grades for 90 percent of bullying victims.[13] Victims often have lower grades than they should. This was more pronounced in junior high and high school than in elementary.[14]

At this stage of the coping path, your child may have experienced some combination of the feelings we have discussed for the earlier stages, as well as secrecy, denial, and desire to withdraw and to avoid school and other social situations. However, there is still a ray of hope that the bullying will end soon.

Trauma

At some point the bullying is considered traumatic by your child. Trauma is defined as an inescapably stressful event that overwhelms the individual's coping mechanisms.[15] At this point victims truly feel overwhelmed. Such a feeling is understand-able. No one should experience the trauma created by bullying.

Toxic Shame and Low Self-Esteem

The child begins to experience more and more shame. This is not healthy shame, the shame that makes one behave more appropriately. It is shame that binds and imprisons the child. It is poisonous shame. James Garbarino has referred to it as *toxic shame*.[16] This shame is no longer just an emotion; it is internal-ized and becomes part of the child's character.

In the books *Healing the Shame That Binds You* and *Homecoming*, John Bradshaw explores the signs and effects of toxic shame, some of which are paraphrased here:[17]

- Toxic shame makes an individual feel fundamentally disgraced.

- Toxic shame makes an individual feel intrinsically worthless.

- Toxic shame causes an individual to feel profoundly humili-ated in her own skin.

- Toxic shame is experienced as the all-pervasive sense that one is flawed and defective as a human being.

- Toxic shame is no longer an emotion that signals our limits; it is a state of being, a core identity.

- Toxic shame gives one a sense of failing and falling short as a human being.

- Toxic shame is like internal bleeding.

- A shame-based person will guard against exposing her inner self to others, but more significantly she will guard against exposing herself to herself.

- Toxic shame is excruciating because it exposes the perceived failure of self to the self.

- The self becomes an entity that can't be trusted; one experiences oneself as untrustworthy.

- Toxic shame is experienced as inner torment, a sickness of the soul.

- Toxic shame is paradoxical and self-generating: one is ashamed about feeling shame.

- People will readily admit guilt, hurt, or fear before they will admit shame.

- Toxic shame is the feeling of being isolated and alone in a complete sense.

- A shame-based person is haunted by a sense of absence and emptiness.

At this point, the child's self-esteem is so damaged, she is blind to her positive characteristics and strengths. In fact, she seeks to protect her self-esteem from further harm. This is often evidenced by an oversensitivity to and misinterpretation of comments and questions from peers and adults. She views questions of concern and interest as personal attacks on her capabilities, as expressions of disappointment and lack of confidence in her.

Toxic shame is so poisonous that the child becomes more doubtful about her own ability to cope with the bullying, more doubtful about adults helping her, and even more doubtful that life and school life will be good to her. A sense of helplessness begins to invade her thoughts.

When your child feels helpless, she may start bullying others. Psychologists say that victims of mistreatment sometimes "identify with the aggressor."[18] She may do this to turn her feelings of helplessness into feelings of power. No one wants to feel helpless. We all prefer to feel powerful, even children.

At this stage of the coping path, your child may have experienced a mixture of hurt and pain, embarrassment, humiliation, intimidation, fear, anxiety, hyperalertness, lack of concentration, confused thinking and poor decision making, fatigue, irritability, impatience, lack of motivation, feelings of inadequacy, inappropriate behavior, initial thoughts of retaliation, entrapment, loneliness, abandonment, rejection, alienation, disappointment, lack of trust in people and life, rejection proneness (expectation of being rejected), secrecy, denial, desire to withdraw and to avoid school as well as other social situations, toxic shame, low self-esteem, and helplessness. There is still some ray of hope that the bullying will end, but the child's sense of helplessness is starting to turn into hopelessness.

Irritability, Anger, and Hostility

As your child travels the hurtful path of bullying, she will become irritable and angry. It is difficult to know which comes first, irritability or anger. She is frequently angry at the bully, the bully's followers, nonresponsive bystanders, and adults who have failed to intervene.[19] This irritability and anger seem to stem from feelings of entrapment, stress, helplessness, and poor self-esteem. Because most children prefer not to have these feelings, your child may repress her anger toward herself; toward those who ignore, encourage, or reinforce the bullying; and toward those who bully her. Gradually this internalized anger moves from being an emotion to being part of the individual's character. During this time, your child may become a bully and have trouble forming new meaningful relationships.

At this stage of the coping path, your child may have experienced a mixture of the feelings associated with earlier stages, as well as increased irritability, anger, and hostility.

There is increased doubt that the bullying will stop, and the sense of hopelessness is overcoming the feeling of helplessness. Life, especially school life, seems to be out of control.

Hopelessness, Anxiety Attacks, Depression, and Posttraumatic Stress Syndrome

If the child doesn't receive the professional assistance she needs, all the feelings she has experienced thus far begin to intensify. In fact, she may exhibit all the signs of posttraumatic stress.

- Sleep problems, nightmares, and waking early
- Impaired memory
- Inability to concentrate
- Hypervigilance (feels like but is not paranoia)
- Jumpiness
- Exaggerated startle response
- Hypersensitivity
- Irritability
- Violent outbursts
- Joint and muscle pains
- Panic attacks
- Fatigue
- Low self-esteem
- Exaggerated feelings of guilt
- Feelings of nervousness and anxiety

She may also have trouble controlling her anger and may even exhibit aggression against herself and others.

At this stage of the coping path, your child may have experienced a mixture of hurt and pain, embarrassment, humiliation, intimidation, fear, anxiety, hyperalertness, lack of concentration, confused thinking and poor decision making, fatigue, irritability, impatience, lack of motivation, feelings of inadequacy, inappropriate behavior, initial thoughts of retaliation, entrapment, loneliness, abandonment, rejection, alienation, disappointment, lack of trust in people and life, rejection proneness (expects to be rejected), secrecy, denial, desire to withdraw and to avoid school as well as other social situations, toxic shame, low self-esteem, helplessness, increased irritability, anger, hostility, hopelessness, anxiety attacks, depression, and possibly posttraumatic stress.

Seeking to Have Needs Met

By the time a child has experienced the previous coping stages, she is desperate to meet her needs for safety, for acceptance, and for a sense of belonging.

The need to belong and to be accepted screams to be met, must be met, will be met. Your child may become desperate to be accepted by her peers, to fit in. If she can't find acceptance in appropriate places, she may seek to have this need met in the wrong places with the wrong people. To find acceptance, she may join a gang. Being mistreated every day makes a child feel very insecure and unsafe. Gangs offer security and a sense of belonging. For some children who do not feel loved at home, the gang offers a "family." Drug groups also offer acceptance, a sense of belonging, and a means of mentally flying away from mistreatment.

Your child may also be at risk of joining a cult or forming her own cult. Cult leaders may seek her out and offer her acceptance, a sense of belonging, and an opportunity to feel valued or important. The ringleader of a vampire student group at one high school in Kentucky said, "If you can't be a jock or a cheerleader, you can always be a vamp." She offered rejected students a place to belong and tried to convince them to kill their parents.

Some bullied children join hate groups. One girl who was rejected by her parents and her peers said she finally found someone who loved her and gave her something important to do. She was talking about a hate group, and the "something important to do" was to hand out hate literature. She had such a great need to feel accepted and valued that she was willing to do something wrong.

Bullied females may seek to get pregnant in order to find acceptance. One sixteen year-old girl said, "I want a baby, not a husband." She was voicing her need to have someone to love and to have someone who would love her unconditionally. She knew the baby would love her, even if she failed her classes, was considered ugly by her peers, and wasn't a cheerleader or popular.

At this stage of the coping path, your child may have experienced a combination of all the feelings of the previous stages, and may now desire to join a gang, drug group, or cult.

Hate and Rage

Your child may have unresolved anger that could turn into hate and rage. Because hate and rage drive the child to ignore rules and laws, they are dangerous enemies. The fear, anger, hate, and hostility of a person who has been bullied fuel the fires of rage, and rage then demands some kind of action.

At this stage, the child has experienced a mixture of hurt and pain, embarrassment, humiliation, fear, anxiety, intimidation, hyperalertness, lack of concentration, confused thinking, poor decision making, fatigue, irritability, impatience, lack of motivation, feelings of inadequacy, initial thoughts of retaliation, inappropriate behavior, entrapment, stress, disappointment, lack of trust in people and life, rejection proneness (expectation of being rejected), secrecy, denial, withdrawal and avoidance, toxic shame, low self-esteem, increased irritability, anger, hostility, hate, and rage.

Choices

When a bullied child feels helpless and her hope has faded, she feels that she has three major choices. These choices sometimes just add to the confusion she feels and place the child in the middle of a dilemma because two of these choices are not consistent with the moral values that children are taught.

Choice 1: Stop the Bullying by Retaliating—Seeking Revenge

Fear is an emotion that seems to live in all the coping stages. One option the victim may consider is to stop the bullying any way she can, regardless of the consequences. She may decide to hurt or even kill the bully. According to Allan N. Schwartz, "Fear is part of the mechanism that allows people to hate and kill those they perceive as the enemy." He says that some victimized people dehumanize those viewed as "them," which makes it easier to kill "them" because they are perceived as not really being human.[20] Michael Carneal, who shot into a prayer group at Heath High School of West Paducah, Kentucky, leaving three dead and five injured, said, "I didn't know who I had shot until I read their names in the newspaper. I knew I would go to prison, but in my mind I was leaving everything behind. I perceived my life as miserable. Nobody loved me and nobody cared." Of course, this wasn't true. His parents loved him very much.

When the victim decides to retaliate, she feels she must equalize the power imbalance between her and the bully or bullies. So she may decide to use a weapon, the element of surprise, or both. One high school girl stabbed a bully in the back with a pencil. One middle school boy stood inside the locker room with a baseball bat. When the bully walked in, he crushed his knee caps. Another middle school boy caught the bully not looking and pushed him. The bully fell, hit his head on a concrete bench, and was killed.

The victim may attack specific individuals or groups that initiated, encouraged, or reinforced the bullying. Or she may strike out at the world, which she has experienced as being full of negative experiences.

At this point, the victim may become focused on herself and focused on protecting other victims. Carneal said, "At the time of the shooting, I thought only about myself, not about the people who would be hurt, or their families, or the community." The young man who retaliated with a baseball bat said, "I just wanted to stop him from bullying me and stop him from bullying others. I didn't want to hurt him seriously."

Choice 2: Self-Harm

It's not natural to think about hurting or killing someone, so the child may choose instead to hurt herself. This is another way to cope with the hurt and to obtain some control over her life. Or the victims may harm themselves by trying to escape their bullying through alcohol and drugs, as described by the young man in the e-mail appearing at the beginning of this chapter. Some victims may engage in self-mutilation. I was visiting a school where three girls asked for a meeting with me. They told me that they were cutting themselves because two boys bullied them every day. Some victims may develop an eating disorder because persistent mistreatment causes them to feel that their life is out of their control. Food offers an easy way for victims to have self-control—unfortunately, in a negative fashion.

Some victims of bullying may think about and even commit suicide. Many times, these thoughts of suicide are spontaneous and temporary. With the right support from adults, these thoughts pass. However, sometimes victims decide they would rather be dead than experience a life of hell. One girl who was bullied by a group of girls decided to escape the problem by hanging herself. Her parents found a suicide note she had written that said she was tired of how the girls were treating her.

Choice 3: Accept and Resolve—Seek Assistance to Stop the Bullying

Instead of retaliating or harming herself, your child may accept her situation and be resolved to seek help. It is a healthy sign to see your child moving from denial and avoidance to confronting the bullying and discussing all aspects of her experience. Your child may even seek the support of a trusted friend or a sibling. Many victims are more willing to tell their siblings than their parents. When your child tells you or a sibling that she is being bullied, take it seriously and treat the problem carefully. Use the suggestions in this book to address the bullying situation before it gets out of hand.

Understanding why some children go from a deep hurt to fear, to overwhelming anxiety, to anger, to hate, to rage, and sometimes to retaliation, self-mutilation, or suicide can help you address your child's problem. Bullying weakens the mind, the heart, the body, and the spirit.

In addition to helping your own child escape from a bullying situation, work with your child's school and community to stop bullying everywhere. Many victimized children are living in darkness. You and I must be the light in that darkness.

KEY MESSAGES

- The path from hurt to revenge starts with persistent mistreatment and embarrassment.

- Victims of bullying sometimes feel defective.

- Anticipating future mistreatment may cause overwhelming anxiety that can dominate a child's thinking and affect her ability to make decisions.

- Victims often have traumatic memories of the bullying, especially when alone.

- It is not uncommon for victims to experience fatigue, which contributes to their irritability, impatience, and inappropriate behavior.

- Victims often feel they are trapped in a situation that will only get worse and last a long time.

- Fear increases when victims feel that they can't trust adults to help them.

- Increased feelings of intimidation and inadequacy diminish self-confidence and lead to feelings of entrapment and fear.

- As anxiety and stress increase, confused thinking increases, and it is not unusual for victims' grades to drop.

- Some victims experience a trust crisis.

- Victims often try to keep their mistreatment a secret and even unconsciously deny that it is happening.

- Victims frequently try to cope with bullies by avoiding them. Therefore, they try to avoid going to school, certain classes, or activities.

- Victims may experience toxic shame.

- Some victims have anxiety attacks, get depressed, and experience posttraumatic stress.

- Victims may seek to meet their need to be accepted and to be safe by joining gangs, cults, hate groups, or drug groups. Or they may turn to drugs, alcohol, and sex.

- The unresolved anger in some victims may turn into hate and rage.

- When efforts to cope have failed, victims feel that they have three choices: self-harm (mutilation, suicide), retaliation, or seeking help from a trusted adult.

- Adults need to identify where victims are on this tragic path of coping with bullying and help children before it's too late.

13

Working with Your Child's School

Dear Dr. Beane:

I have a thirteen-year-old daughter who is being bullied at school. Her self-esteem is very low and she has been contemplating suicide. I spoke with the school and they have informed me that there is money in the school's budget for a Safer Schools program, but they have not found a way to introduce it to our schools. Therefore, I am respectfully pleading, begging, whatever is necessary, for you to bring your program to our schools and assist our school board with setting the program in place. Please give my request serious consideration and place it high on your priority list. My daughter's life depends on it.

In order to make our schools bully free, parents, school personnel, students, and community representatives must work together. Every child has the right to feel safe at school. Therefore, because bullying occurs to some degree in every school and starts around age three, an anti-bullying program should be implemented at every level in every school. The e-mail message above expresses the sense of urgency and passion needed to establish such a program. Parents have an important role to play and often encourage the implementation of a program. For an anti-bullying program to be effective, your involvement and support are needed. Here are a few suggestions for you:

• Ask your child's principal (or teacher or school counselor) if there is a "Parent's Pledge" you can sign to indicate your support of their anti-bullying efforts. If there is, tell them you want to sign it and support the program. Tell them you also want to attend school meetings and activities focusing on the prevention of bullying.

• When your child brings home information and homework assignments related to bullying, review the material with him. Make a copy of the homework or make a few notes regarding the information. Occasionally, during family meetings or casual conversations, remind your child of the information gained from doing the homework. Reinforce what is taught at school.

• Volunteer to supervise high-risk areas (such as playground, hallways, stairwells, cafeteria, bathrooms, parking lots, bus stops, and so on). These are the areas where bullying occurs most often because of a lack of adequate adult supervision. Also indicate your willingness to be trained to effectively supervise the area(s) assigned to you.

• Support the anti-bullying policies of your child's school. If the school or school system has a policy, ask for a copy of it. Go over the policy with your children and make sure they understand your support of the policy. Tell them that if they ever bully anyone directly or as a follower, you will support the school's use of consequences and that additional consequences could be applied at home.

• Help your child's school develop anti-bullying bulletin boards for the classrooms and for hallways. Resources for such bulletin boards can be found at www.bullyfree.com. Such displays communicate that the school is serious about preventing and stopping bullying.

- Encourage your school to use reporting or "bully boxes" and a telephone hotline so that students can anonymously report mistreatment. Some schools have even established anonymous e-mail systems for this type of reporting. Or teachers can place boxes on their desks where students can report anything, including their observation of someone displaying a positive character trait. Students often feel more comfortable with this kind of reporting.

- Encourage your child's school to add structure to recess or to schedule different times for recess for older and younger students. Adding structure can mean requiring students to plan all their activities before they go to recess. This is one way of ensuring that all students are included and that no one student is trying to dominate the decisions on the playground. The school could also restrict older students to a certain area of the playground. Certain areas, such as behind buildings, could be marked as off-limits by spraying paint on the ground next to the buildings to indicate the boundaries of the play area.

- Encourage the school to purchase safe, good-quality, interesting outdoor equipment for the playground. Research indicates that when the equipment is interesting and in good condition, it can help reduce behavior problems on the playground. When children are bored, there is more conflict.

- Encourage your child's school to provide an assembly program for students and to provide anti-bullying training for all school personnel. A school assembly program is only the first step. It should always be followed by training for all school personnel. Many times, school assembly programs are scheduled by the school counselor, or the principal assigns the task to a teacher. Most school districts have a staff or professional development coordinator who schedules such training. When awareness training is provided, all school personnel, including school nurses, secretaries, custodians, and bus drivers, need to attend the meeting. Some training sessions will be most appropriate for teachers, counselors and psychologists, and administrators. Visit www.bullyfree.com to see a description of the different types of training that could be offered.

• Encourage your child's school to purchase resources about bullying—books for teachers, counselors, students, and parents; videos; posters; and pamphlets. Bullying has been a hot topic, and several companies are developing products that can be used by schools. One effective program is our Bully Free Program (www.bullyfree.com).

• Encourage your child's school to purchase and install surveillance equipment (video cameras, photo cameras, metal detectors, and curved mirrors) for playgrounds, buses, and other areas lacking adult supervision. Some schools have even installed video cameras in the classroom.

• Encourage your child's school to consider requiring school uniforms. Uniforms will not stop bullying, but they eliminate one thing that students are teased about: clothing. Uniforms have also been known to reduce discipline problems in schools.

• Encourage the school to hire school resource officers; they can help supervise high-risk areas and develop meaningful relationships with students.

• Work with other parents in the community and establish "safe places" between children's homes and the school. Some parents have also established a telephone network so that children can call other parents for help if they cannot contact their parents.

• Ask the school to examine its use of school counselors or to hire more so that they can use their time to counsel students who have problems. Too often counselors serve as assistant principals. Many counselors are very involved in the teaching process and often visit classrooms to conduct lessons about bullying.

• Ask the school to establish a system for erasing hurtful graffiti on the walls of the school. Usually the custodian is given this responsibility. Whoever is given this responsibility should keep a log of comments that degrade or threaten the safety of others.

• Ask the school to establish a school "welcome wagon" program or committee for new students. Volunteer to help develop the program. The committee should include students who welcome and befriend new students. Committee members could introduce new students to school personnel and others as well as accompanying them to school events.

• Ask the school to hold meetings with groups of students, as well as parents, to discuss bullying and other school safety issues. Offer to help coordinate or supervise these meetings. You could also ask different groups of parents to furnish the refreshments. Prior to the meeting, ask a parent to be prepared to record the names of those in attendance as well as the comments, recommendations, and decisions made at the meeting.

• An anti-bullying program cannot be successful without your support, encouragement, and involvement. Seek to be involved in the efforts of your child's school. If your child's school system needs assistance, ask them to contact me at abeane@bullyfree.com.

KEY MESSAGES

• In order to make schools bully free, parents, school personnel, students, and community representatives must work together.

• Volunteer to supervise high-risk areas (hallways, playgrounds, buses and bus stops, cafeteria, parking lots, stairwells, locker rooms, commons areas, and so on).

• Support the anti-bullying policies of your child's school.

• Encourage your child's school to have an anti-bullying program.

Conclusion

Dear Dr. Beane:

You don't know me, but I thought I should contact you and let you know that your program saved my son's life. Thank you and may God bless you!

The preceding e-mail summarizes what it is all about for me. I hope this book will be helpful to you and your family and that it saves more children from the pain of bullying. Continue to look for good books that can help you. You will also find a wealth of helpful material on the Internet. The following is only a sampling of web sites you will find informative and useful

Bully Free Systems, LLC
www.bullyfree.com

Bullying.org
www.bullying.org

Stop Bullying Now
www.stopbullyingnow.hrsa.gov

Bullystoppers.com
www.bullystoppers.com

Students Unified with Parents and Educators to Resolve Bullying (SUPERB)
www.nochildfearschool.org/resources.htm

National Parent Teacher Association
www.pta.org/programs/sycsch.htm

Dealing with Bullies from the Safe Child Organization
www.safechild.org/bullies.htm

Bullying Information for Parents and Teachers
www.lfcc.on.ca/bully.htm

Take Action Against Bullying
www.bullybeware.com

Office of Juvenile Justice and Delinquency Prevention (OJJDP)
www.ojjdp.ncjrs.org/jjbulletin/9804/bullying.html
http://ojjdp/fs200127.pdf
http://ncjrs.org/pdf-files/167888.pdf

You know your child better than anyone, so you should decide what strategies are best for your child and family. As mentioned throughout this book, your involvement in a bullying prevention program at your child's school is critical. Please don't hesitate to voice your interest in helping the school establish such a program. Help me spread the good news that there is hope for the victims of bullying and that there is hope in helping children who bully to change.

I hope your child is bully free. I hope his life has been filled with health, peace, and happiness. I hope this book has brought light into the darkness. I hope your child will bring light into the darkness of others.

Appendix A
Child Review Questions

- What are my child's relationships like?
- Does my child spend a lot of time alone?
- Does he have at least one best friend?
- Does he respect my authority?
- What is his attitude toward school?
- Is he doing well in school?
- Does he show me respect?
- How is his physical health?
- Does my child sleep too much or too little?
- How is his emotional health?
- Does my child seem sad, tired, restless, or out of sorts?
- Does my child have frequent outbursts of shouting, complaining, or crying?
- How is his spiritual health?
- Is he obedient?
- Does he have to be in control? Is he controlling?
- Is able to appropriately compromise?
- Does he seek the attention of others?
- Does he feel good about himself?
- Does my child show signs of drug or alcohol use?
- Does he lack self-confidence?
- Are his values consistent with mine?
- Does he have any special areas of interest?

- How does he spend his leisure time?
- What does he feel passionate about?
- Does he understand that his behavior has consequences?
- Does he understand how his behavior has an impact others?
- Who is his favorite person and why?
- What does he most worry about?
- What does he like most about himself?
- What does he like least about himself?
- What does he want to do when he grows up?
- What type of music does he listen to most?
- What television shows does he like most?
- What Internet sites does he visit?
- Does he mistreat others?
- Do others mistreat him?
- Does my child talk about death or suicide?

Appendix B
Mental Health Resources

National Institute of Mental Health
Office of Communications
Information Resources and Inquiries Branch
6001 Executive Boulevard, Rm. 8184, MSC 9663
Bethesda, MD 20892-9663
(301) 443-4513
Mental Health FAX 4U: (301) 443-5158
E-mail: nimhinfo@nih.gov
NIMH home page: www.nimh.nih.gov

American Academy of Child and Adolescent Psychiatry
3615 Wisconsin Avenue, N.W.
Washington, DC 20016
(202) 966-7300
www.aacap.org

American Psychiatric Association
1400 K Street, N.W.
Washington, DC 2005
(202) 682-6000
www.psych.org

American Psychological Association
750 First Street, N.E.
Washington, DC 20002
(202) 336-5500
www.apa.org

Child & Adolescent Bipolar Foundation
1187 Willmette Avenue, PMB #331
Willmette, IL 60091
(847) 256-8525
www.bpkids.org

National Alliance for the Mentally Ill (NAMI)
Colonial Place Three
2107 Wilson Blvd., Suite 300
Arlington, VA 22201
Phone: 1-800-950-NAMI (6264) or (703) 524-7600
www.nami.org

Depression & Bipolar Support Alliance (DBSA)
730 N. Franklin St., #501
Chicago, IL 60610-7224
(312) 988-1150
Fax: (312) 642-7243
www.DBSAlliance.org

National Mental Health Association (NMHA)
2001 N. Beauregard Street, 12th floor
Alexandria, VA 22311
Phone: 1-800-969-6942 or (703) 684-7722
TTY: 800-443-5959
www.nmha.org

NOTES

Chapter One

1. Roberts, 2006.
2. Olweus, 1978.
3. Cited in Cassidy, 1999.
4. Olweus, 1978.
5. Besag, 1989.
6. Elliott, 1991.
7. Teachsafeschools.org, 2007.
8. National Youth Violence Prevention Resource Center, 2006.
9. Teachsafeschools.org, n.d.
10. Teachsafeschools.org, n.d.
11. Olweus, 1993.
12. American Medical Association, n.d.

Chapter Three

1. Cash and Pruzinsky, 2002.
2. Aharon et al., 2001.
3. Olweus, 1994.
4. Wirth and Schultheis, 2007.
5. Byrne, 1994.

6. Clark, 1993.

7. "Research on the Effects of Media Violence," 2007.

8. "Research on the Effects of Media Violence," 2007.

9. "Research on the Effects of Media Violence," 2007.

10. Mueller, 1999.

11. "Can a Video Game Lead to Murder?" 2005.

12. Radio Advertising Bureau, 2002.

13. Radio Advertising Bureau, 2002.

14. Radio Advertising Bureau, 2002.

15. Terry and Jackson, 1985.

16. Shaughnessy, 2007.

17. Powdermaker and Storen, 1944.

18. Sanford, 1995.

19. Sanford, 1995.

20. Olweus, 1995.

21. Olweus, 1993.

22. Rigby, 1996.

23. O'Moore and Kirkham, 2001.

24. Cited in Garbarino, 1999.

25. Stephenson and Smith, 1991; Elliott, 1994.

Chapter Four

1. Dobson, 1988, p. 38.

2. Dobson, 1988, pp. 32–33.

3. Ziglar, 1989.

4. Dobson, 1988.

5. Ginott, 1969.

6. Ziglar, 1989.

7. Tripp, 1995.

8. Federal Communications Commission, 2007.

9. Shifrin, 1998.

10. Grossman, 1999.

11. Elliott, 1996.

12. Grossman, 1999.

13. "Sex and Violence … and It's on the Radio," 2005.

14. National Crime Prevention Council, 2007.

Chapter Five

1. "SVRC Briefing Paper: Bullying," 2001.

Chapter Six

1. Dellasega and Nixon, 2003.

2. Dellasega and Nixon, 2003.

3. National Center for Posttraumatic Stress Disorder, 2007.

4. Weissman and others, 1999.

5. American Academy of Experts in Traumatic Stress, 2003.

Chapter Seven

1. Belsey, n.d.

2. Van Auken, 2005.

3. Van Auken, 2005.

4. Office of the Attorney General, Commonwealth of Kentucky, 2007.

5. Office of the Attorney General, Commonwealth of Kentucky, 2007.

6. Center for Safe and Responsible Internet Use, 2005.

7. Stopcyberbullying.org, n.d.

8. Agatston, 2007.

9. Manke, 2005.

10. Office of the Attorney General, Commonwealth of Kentucky, 2007.

11. Office of the Attorney General, Commonwealth of Kentucky, 2007.

12. Office of the Attorney General, Commonwealth of Kentucky, 2007.

13. Belsey, n.d.

Chapter Eleven

1. Olweus, 1993.

Chapter Twelve

1. Miller and Beane, 1999.

2. Marr and Field, 2001.

3. Simmons, 2002.

4. Miller and Beane, 1999.

5. Marr and Field, 2001, p. xiii.

6. Mottet and Thweatt, 1997.

7. Mottet and Thweatt, 1997, p. 245.

8. Miller and Beane, 1999.

9. Marr and Field, 2001, p. 245.

10. Ross, 1996.

11. Kochenderfer and Ladd, 1996.

12. Banks, 1997.

13. Ross, 1996.

14. Olweus, 1995.

15. van der Kolk and Fishler, 1995.

16. Garbarino, 1999.

17. Garbarino, 1999, pp. 58–59.

18. Schwartz, 2006.

19. Miller, Beane, and Kraus, 1998.

20. Schwartz, 2006.

BIBLIOGRAPHY

Agatston, P. (2007). Help tips for reporting offensive profiles to social networking sites (compiled). Available at www.cyberbullyhelp.com/Help%20Tips%20for%20Reporting%20Offensive%20Profiles.pdf.

Aharon, I., Etcoff, N., Ariely, D., Chabris, C. F., O'Connor, E., & Breiter, H. C. (2001). Beautiful faces have variable reward value: fMRI and behavioral evidences. *Neuron, 32,* 537–551.

American Academy of Experts in Traumatic Stress. (2003). *A practical guide for crisis response in our schools* (5th ed.). Commack, NY: Author.

American Academy of Pediatrics. (2003). Media alert: AAP addresses Colorado shooting. Retrieved July 16, 2007, from www.aap.org. (This web page no longer available.)

American Psychiatric Association. (1994). *Diagnostic and statistical manual of mental disorders* (4th ed.). Washington, DC: American Psychiatric Publishing.

Arp, D., & Arp, C. (2003). *Answering the eight cries of the spirited child.* West Monroe, LA: Howard.

Atlas, R. S., & Pepler, D. J. (1998). Observations of bullying in the classroom. *Journal of Educational Research, 92*(2), 86–99.

Banks, R. (1997). *Bullying in schools* (Report No. EDDY-PS-97-17). Champaign, IL: ERIC Clearinghouse on Elementary and Early Childhood Education. (ERIC Document Reproduction Service No. ED 407154)

Beane, A. L. (1999). *The bully free classroom.* Minneapolis, MN: Free Spirit.

Beane, A. L. (2003). *What are the possible causes of bullying?* Murray, KY: Bully Free Systems.

Beane, A. L. (2003). *What is the nature of bullying?* Murray, KY: Bully Free Systems.

Beane, A. L. (2003). *Why are some victims of bullying retaliating?* Murray, KY: Bully Free Systems.

Beane, A. L. (2003). *Why should bullying be prevented and stopped?* Murray, KY: Bully Free Systems.

Beaudoin, M.-N., & Taylor, M. (2004). *Breaking the culture of bullying and disrespect, grades K-8.* Thousands Oaks, CA: Corwin Press.

Belsey, B. Cyberbullying: An emerging threat to the "always on" generation. Retrieved July 17, 2007, from http://cyberbullying.ca/pdf/Cyberbullying_Article_by_Bill_Belsey.pdf.

Benson, P. L., Galbraith, J., & Espeland, P. (1994). *What kids need to succeed.* Minneapolis, MN: Free Spirit.

Besag, V. E. (1989). *Bullies and victims in schools.* Milton Keynes, U.K.: Open University Press.

Birmaher, B., Brent, D. A., & Benson, R. S. (1998). Summary of the practice parameters for the assessment and treatment of children and adolescents with depressive disorders. *Journal of the American Academy of Child and Adolescent Psychiatry, 37,* 1234–1238.

Birmaher, B., Ryan, N. D., Williamson, D. E., Brent, D. A., Kaufman, J., Dahl, R. E., Perel, J., & Nelson, B. (1996). Childhood and adolescent depression: A review of the past ten years. Part I. *Journal of the American Academy of Child and Adolescent Psychiatry, 35,* 1427–1439.

Bluestein, J. (1997). *The parent's little book of lists.* Deerfield Beach, FL: Health Communications.

Bowman, D. H. (2001, May 2). Survey of students documents the extent of bullying. *Education Week, 20*(33), 11.

Bullying: No Way! (2004). Socioeconomic status. Available at www.bullyingnoway.com.au/issues/socioeconomic.shtml.

Byrne, B. (1993). *Coping with bullying in schools.* Blackrock, Ireland: Columba Press.

Byrne, B. (1994). *Bullying: A community approach.* Blackrock, Ireland: Columba Press.

Cairns, R. B., Cairns, B. D., Neckenman, H. J., Gest, S., & Gariepy, J. L. (1988). Peer networks and aggressive behavior: Social support or social rejection? *Developmental Psychology, 24,* 815–823.

Can a video game lead to murder? (2005, June 19). CBS News. Available at www.cbsnews.com/stories/2005/06/17/60minutes/main702599.shtml.

Cash, T. F. & Pruzinsky, T., eds. (2002). *Body image: a handbook of theory, research, and clinical practice.* New York: Guilford Press.

Cassidy, S. (1999, December 24). Beware the "pure bully" who never takes time off. *Times Educational Supplement,* p. 3.

Center for Safe and Responsible Internet Use. (2005). A parent's guide to cyberbullying and cyberthreats. Available at www.nisd.net/webwarning/pdf/cbctparents.pdf.

Clark, C. S. (1993, March 26). TV violence. *CQ Researcher, 3*(12), 167–187.

Coughlin, P. (2007). *No more jellyfish, chickens, or wimps: Raising secure, assertive kids in a tough world.* Minneapolis, MN: Bethany House.

Crosbie, S. (2003, March 31). When bullying reaches into cyberspace. *Kingston Whig-Standard.* Available at www.cyberbullying.ca/whig_standard_march_31_2003.html.

Dellasega, C., & Nixon, C. (2003). *Girl wars: Twelve strategies that will end female bullying*. New York: Simon & Schuster.

Dobson, J. (1988). *Dare to discipline*. Wheaton, IL: Tyndale House.

Elliott, M. (1991). Bullies, victims, signs, solutions. In M. Elliott (Ed.), *Bullying: A practical guide to coping for schools* (pp. 8–14). London: Longman.

Elliott, M. (1994). *Keeping safe: A practical guide to talking with children*. London: Hodder and Stoughton.

Elliott, M. (1996). *501 ways to be a good parent*. London: Hodder and Stoughton.

Espelage, D. L., & Swearer, S. M. (Eds.). (2004). *Bullying in American schools: A social-ecological perspective on prevention and intervention*. Mahwah, NJ: Erlbaum.

Federal Communications Commission. Television viewing (fact sheet). Available at http://fcc.gov/Bureaus/Mass_Media/Factsheets/factvchip.html.

Fleming, J. E., & Offord, D. R. (1990). Epidemiology of childhood depressive disorders: A critical review. *Journal of the American Academy of Child and Adolescent Psychiatry, 29,* 571–580.

Fox, J., Elliott, D., Kerlikowske, R., Newman, S., & Christeson, W. (2003). *Bullying prevention is crime prevention*. Washington, DC: Fight Crime: Invest in Kids.

Freedman, J. S. (2002). *Easing the teasing*. Chicago: Contemporary Books.

Fried, S., & Fried, P. (1996). *Bullies and victims: Helping your child survive the schoolyard battlefield*. New York: Evans.

Garbarino, J. (1999). *Lost boys*. New York: Free Press.

Garbarino, J., & deLara, E. (2002). *And words can hurt forever*. New York: Free Press.

Garrity, C., Baris, M., & Porter, W. (2000). *Bully proofing your child: A parent's guide*. Longmont, CO: Sopris West.

Garrity, C., Jens, K., Porter, W., Sager, N., & Short-Camilli, C. (1996). *Bully-proofing your school: A comprehensive approach for elementary schools*. Longmont, CO: Sopris West.

Geller, B., & Luby, J. (1997). Child and adolescent bipolar disorder: A review of the past ten years. *Journal of the American Academy of Child and Adolescent Psychiatry, 36,* 1168–1176.

Giannetti, C. C., & Sagarese, M. (2001). *Cliques: Eight steps to help your child survive the social jungle*. New York: Broadway Books.

Ginott, H. G. (1969). *Between parent and teen-ager*. New York: Avon Books.

Glenn, H. S., & Nelsen, J. (1989). *Raising self-reliant children in a self-indulgent world*. Rocklin, CA: Prima.

Greenbaum, S., Turner, B., & Stephens, R. (1989). *Set straight on bullies*. Malibu, CA: Pepperdine University Press.

Grossman, D. (1999). *Stop teaching our kids to kill*. New York: Crown.

Hawker, D.S.J., & Boulton, M. J. (2000). Twenty years' research on peer victimization and psychosocial maladjustment: A meta-analytic review of cross-sectional studies. *Journal of Child Psychology and Psychiatry and Allied Disciplines*, *41*, 441–455.

Hazler, R. J., Hoover, J. H., & Oliver, R. L. (1991). Student perceptions of victimization by bullies in school. *Journal of Humanistic Education and Development*, *29*, 143–150.

Hoover, J. H., & Oliver, R. L. (1996). *The bullying prevention handbook: A guide for principals, teachers, and counselors*. Bloomington, IN: National Educational Service.

Hoover, J. H., Oliver, R. L., & Hazler, R. J. (1992). Bullying: Perceptions of adolescent victims in the midwestern U.S.A. *School Psychology International*, *13*, 5–16.

Hoyert, D. L., Kochanek, K. D., & Murphy, S. L. (1999). Deaths: Final data for 1997. *National Vital Statistics Reports*, *47*(19). DHHS Publication No. (PHS) 99-1120. Hyattsville, MD: National Center for Health Statistics. Available at www.cdc.gov/nchs/data/nvsr/nvsr47/nvs47_19.pdf.

i-SAFEAmerica. (2005, May). Beware of the cyber bully. Available at www.isafe.org/imgs/pdf/education/CyberBullying.pdf.

Kidscape. *You can beat bullying: A guide for young people*. London: Kidscape.

Klerman, G. L., & Weissman, M. M. (1989). Increasing rates of depression. *Journal of the American Medical Association*, *261*, 2229–2235.

Kochenderfer, B. J., & Ladd, G. W. (1996). Peer victimization: Cause of consequence of school maladjustment? *Child Development*, *67*, 1305–1317.

Kovacs, M. (1997). Psychiatric disorders in youths with IDDM: Rates and risk factors. *Diabetes Care*, *20*(1), 36–44.

Kovacs, M., Feinberg, T. L., Crouse-Novak, M. A., Paulauskas, S. L., & Finkelstein, R. (1984). Depressive disorders in childhood. I. A longitudinal prospective study of characteristics and recovery. *Archives of General Psychiatry*, *41*, 229–237.

Kreidler, W. J. (1996). Smart ways to handle kids who pick on others. *Instructor*, *105*(2), 70–74.

Leonard, W. M. (1988). *A sociological perspective of sport* (3rd ed.). New York: Macmillan.

Lewinsohn, P. M., Rohde, P., & Seeley, J. R. (1998). Major depressive disorder in older adolescents: Prevalence, risk factors, and clinical implications. *Clinical Psychology Review*, *18*, 765–794.

Locke, D. C. (1992). *Increasing multicultural understanding: A comprehensive model*. Thousand Oaks, CA: Sage.

Manke, B. (2005, March). The impact of cyberbullying. Available at www.mindoh.com/docs/BM_Cyberbullying.pdf.

Many students engage in bullying. (1999). Available at www.applesforhealth. com/bullying1.html.

Marr, N., & Field, T. (2001). *Bullycide: Death at playtime*. Didcot, England: Success Unlimited.

Maudlin, K. (2002). *Sticks and stones*. Nashville, TN: Nelson.

McDill, S. R., Jr., & Stephens, R. D. (1993). *Raising safety-smart kids*. Nashville, TN: Nelson.

Middleton-Moz, J., & Zawadski, M. L. (2002). *Bullies: From the playground to the boardroom*. Deerfield Beach, FL: Health Communications.

Miller, T. W., & Beane, A. L. (1999). Clinical impact on child victims of bullying in the schools. *Directions*, 9(10), 126.

Miller, T. W., Beane, A. L., & Kraus, R. F. (1998). Clinical and cultural issues in diagnosing and treating child victims of abuse. *Child Psychiatry and Human Development, 29*(1), 30–31.

Monroe, S. M., Rohde, P., Seeley, J. R., & Lewinsohn, P. M. (1999). Life events and depression in adolescence: Relationship loss as a prospective risk factor for first onset of major depressive disorder. *Journal of Abnormal Psychology, 108*, 606–614.

Mottet, T. P., & Thweatt, K. S. (1997). The relationship between peer teasing, self-esteem, and affect for school. *Communication Research Reports, 14*, 241–248.

Mueller, W. (1999). *Understanding today's youth culture (For parents, teachers, and youth leaders)*. Wheaton, IL: Tyndale House.

National Center for Posttraumatic Stress Disorder. (2007). Frequently asked questions. Available at www.ncptsd.va.gov/ncmain/ncdocs/fact_shts/ fs_faqs_on_ptsd.html.

National Crime Prevention Council. Protect children from gun violence. (2007). Available at www.ncpc.org/topics/by-audience/parents/guns.

National Institute of Mental Health. (2000, September). Depression in children and adolescents: A fact sheet for physicians. (NIH Publication No. 00-4744). Bethesda, MD: National Institute of Mental Health. Available at www.athealth.com/Consumer/disorders/ ChildDepression.html.

National Youth Violence Prevention Resource Center. (2006). Bullying. Available at www.safeyouth.org/scripts/teens/bullying.asp.

Newman, K. S., Fox, C., Harding, D. J., Mehta, J., & Roth, W. (2004). *Rampage: The social roots of school shootings*. New York: Basic Books.

Office of the Attorney General, Commonwealth of Kentucky. (2007). "Cyberbullying." Available at http://ag.ky.gov/cybersafety/ cyberbullying.htm.

Olweus, D. (1978). *Aggression in schools: Bullies and whipping boys*. Washington, D.C.: Hemisphere.

Olweus, D. (1993). *Bullying at school: What we know and what we can do.* Cambridge, MA: Blackwell.

Olweus, D. (1994). Bullying at school: Facts and effects of a school-based intervention program. *Journal of Child Psychiatry, 35*(7), 1171–1190.

Olweus, D. (1995). Bullying or peer abuse at school: Facts and intervention. *Current Directions in Psychological Science, 4*(6), 196–200.

O'Moore, M., & Kirkham, C. (2001). Self-esteem and its relationship to bullying behavior. *Aggressive Behavior, 27,* 269–283.

Parsons, L. (2005). *Bullied teacher, bullied student.* Markham, Ontario: Pembroke.

Pepler, D. J., Craig, W. M., & Roberts, W. (1998). Observations of aggressive and nonaggressive children on the school playground. *Merrill-Palmer Quarterly, 44*(1), 55–76.

Pepler, D. J., Craig, W. M., Ziegler, S., & Charach, A. (1994). An evaluation of an anti-bullying intervention in Toronto schools. *Canadian Journal of Community Mental Health, 13,* 95–110.

Peretti, F. (2000). *The wounded spirit.* Nashville, TN: Word.

Powdermaker, H., & Storen, H. F. (1944). *Probing our prejudices: A unit for high school students.* New York: HarperCollins.

Radio Advertising Bureau. (2002). *Radio marketing guide and fact book for advertisers* (2002-2003 ed.). New York: Author.

Research on the effects of media violence. (2007). Media Awareness Network. Available at www.media-awareness.ca/english/issues/violence/effects_media_violence.cfm.

Rigby, K. (1996). *Bullying in schools and what to do about it.* Melbourne: Acer.

Roberts, W. B., Jr. (2006). *Bullying from both sides.* Thousand Oaks, CA: Corwin Press.

Ross, D. M. (1996). Childhood bullying and teasing: What school personnel, other professionals, and parents can do. Alexandria, VA: American Counseling Association.

Ryan, N. D., Puig-Antich, J., Ambrosini, P., Rabinovich, H., Robinson, D., Nelson, B., Iyengar, S., & Twomey, J. (1987). The clinical picture of major depression in children and adolescents. *Archives of General Psychiatry, 44,* 854–861.

Sanford, D. (1995). *How to answer tough questions kids ask.* Nashville, TN: Nelson.

Scaglione, J., & Scaglione, A. R. (2006). *Bully-proofing children: A practical, hands-on guide to stop bullying.* Lanham, MD: Rowman & Littlefield.

Schoolyard bullying goes high-tech. (2003, July 29). *Paducah Sun.*

Schwartz, A. N. (2006). Hatred, terrorism and trauma. Available at www.mentalhelp.net/poc/view_doc.php?type=doc&id=11055&cn=220.

Sex and violence … and it's on the radio. (2005, February 3). *Today.* Available at www.msnbc.msn.com/id/6901467/.

Shaffer, D., & Craft, L. (1999). Methods of adolescent suicide prevention. *Journal of Clinical Psychiatry, 60*(Suppl. 2), 70–74, 75–76, 113–116.

Shaffer, D., Gould, M. S., Fisher, P., Trautman, P., Moreau, D., Kleinman, M., & Flory, M. (1996). Psychiatric diagnosis in child and adolescent suicide. *Archives of General Psychiatry, 53,* 339–348.

Sharp, S., & Smith, P. K. (Eds.). *Tackling bullying in your school.* New York: Routledge.

Shaughnessy, M. F. (2007, June 21). An interview with Chuck Hellman, author of LuckySports, the Bully Series. EdNews.org. Available at www.ednews.org/articles/13259/1/An-Interview-with-Chuck-Hellman-Author-of-LuckySports-The-Bully-Series/Page1.html.

Shifrin, D. (1998, August). Three-year study documents nature of television violence. *AAP News, 14*(8), 23.

Simmons, R. (2002). *Odd girl out: The hidden culture of aggression in girls.* San Diego: Harcourt.

Spaide, D. (1995). *Teaching your kids to care.* New York: Carol.

Stephenson, P., & Smith, D. (1994). Why some schools don't have bullies. In M. Elliott (Ed.), *Bullying: A practical guide to coping for schools.* London: Longman.

Stopcyberbullying.org. (n.d.). Stop cyberbullying. Available at www.stopcyberbullying.org/parents/guide.html.

Sullivan, K., Cleary, M., & Sullivan, G. (2005). *Bullying in secondary schools: What it looks like and how to manage it.* London: Chapman.

SVRC briefing paper: Bullying. (2001, September). Available at www.svrc.net/Files/Bullying.pdf.

Teachsafeschools.org. (n.d.). How widespread is bullying? Available at www.teachsafeschools.org/bully_menu1.html#4.

Terry, P. C., & Jackson, J. J. (1985). The determinants and control of violence in sport. *Quest, 37*(1), 27–37.

Thompson, M., & Cohen, L. J., with Grace, C. O. *Mom, they're teasing me: Helping your child solve social problems.* New York: Ballantine Books.

Tripp, T. (1995). *Shepherding a child's heart.* Wapwallopen, PA: Shepherd Press.

U.S. Department of Education. (2007). Exploring the nature and prevention of bullying. Available at www.ed.gov/admins/lead/safety/training/bullying/bullying_pg9.html.

Van Auken, E. (2005, March). Behind the screen: Is there a bully in the house? Available at www.mindoh.com/docs/EVA_Cyberbullying.pdf.

van der Kolk, B. A., & Fishler, R. (1995). Dissociation and the fragmentary nature of traumatic memories: Overview and exploratory study. *Journal of Traumatic Stress, 8,* 505–525. Available at www.trauma-pages.com/a/vanderk2.htm.

Weinhold, B., & Weinhold, J. (1998). Conflict resolution: The partnership way in schools. *Counseling and Human Development, 30*(7), 1–12.

Weissman, M. M., Wolk, S., Goldstein, R. B., Moreau, D., Adams, P., Greenwald, S., Klier, C. M., Ryan, N. D., Dahl, R. E., & Wickramaratne, P. (1999). Depressed adolescents grown up. *Journal of the American Medical Association, 281,* 1701–1713.

Wirth, M. M., & Schultheis, O. C. (2007). Basal testosterone moderates responses to anger faces in humans. *Physiology and Behavior, 90,* 496–505.

Ziglar, Z. (1989). *Raising positive kids in a negative world.* New York: Ballantine Books.

Zolten, K., & Long, N. (1997). Family meetings. Center for Effective Parenting. Available at www.parenting-ed.org/handout3/Discipline%20and%20Intervention%20Strategies/family_meetings.htm.

INDEX